THE QUEEN

ALSO BY A.N. WILSON

THE QUEEN

A . N . WILSON

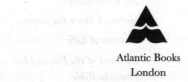

Atlantic Books
London

First published in hardback in Great Britain in 2016 by
Atlantic Books, an imprint of Atlantic Books Ltd.

Sir Max Beerbohm, 'Ballade Tragique a Double Refrain',
in *The Oxford Book of Satirical Verse*, ed. by Geoffrey Grigson
(OUP, 1980), reproduced by permission of Penguin Random House.
Philip Larkin, '1952-1977' and 'Annus Mirabilis', in *The Complete
Poems* (Faber, 2012), reproduced by permission of the Society of
Authors. Sir John Betjeman, 'Death of King George V', in *Continual
Dew* (Hodder, 1937), reproduced by permission of Hodder &
Stoughton Ltd. Christopher Logue, 'I Shall Vote Labour', in the
New Statesman (1966), reproduced by permission of the *New Statesman*.

Every effort has been made to trace or contact all copyright-holders.
The publishers will be pleased to make good any omissions or rectify
any mistakes brought to their attention
at the earliest opportunity.
10 9 8 7 6 5 4 3 2 1

A CIP catalogue record for this book is available
from the British Library.

Hardback ISBN 978 1 78649 068 1
E-book ISBN 978 1 78649 069 8

Designed by Carrdesignstudio.com
Printed and bound by CPI Group (UK) Ltd, Croydon, CR0 4YY

Atlantic Books
An imprint of Atlantic Books Ltd
Ormond House
26–27 Boswell Street
London WC1N 3JZ

For M

CONTENTS

I

IN PRAISE OF DULLNESS

'I don't fully understand her, but that's part of her secret'

ROBERT RUNCIE[1]

The great achievement of Elizabeth II's grandfather, King George V, was to make the British monarchy dull. There had been some danger, during the short reign of his father, Edward VII, that things might get 'interesting'. Not only had Edward the Caresser lived a shameless life, with mistresses galore, but he had also openly and independently indulged in European politics. The *Entente Cordiale* between his country and France was largely his creation, locking Great Britain into treaty obligations – about going to war in the event of another conflict between France and Britain's natural allies and cousins the Germans – that had catastrophic consequences. His diplomatic trip to Paris in 1903 was the last visit abroad by a British sovereign undertaken without ministerial approval.[2]

George V was kept on a much tighter rein, both by his wife and by his Prime Ministers. He was also, luckily for the British Constitution's sake, a much duller dog. His official biographer, Harold Nicolson, exclaimed with self-pity in his diary, 'for seventeen years in fact he did nothing at all but kill animals and stick in stamps'.[3] Sophisticated people found plenty to mock about George V. He was small, and peppery. At the opening of the Tate Gallery extension, he stood before the French Impressionists and called out to the Queen, 'Here's something to make you laugh, May.' In the National Gallery, he had shaken his stick at a Cézanne.[4] At his Silver Jubilee in 1935, he and Queen Mary went to St Paul's Cathedral, where, of course, there was a large gathering of clergy. 'A wonderful service,' the King said afterwards to the Dean. 'The Queen and I are most grateful. Just one thing wrong with it – too many parsons getting in the way.'[5]

Yet, the enormous crowds who filled the streets of London to see their King Emperor on that day moved him, and – for he was a modest man – surprised him. That night, broadcasting to the nation via the relatively new-fangled invention of the wireless, he said, in his strange, cocknified voice, 'I can only say to you, my very dear people, that the Queen and I thank you from the depth of our hearts for all the loyalty and – may I say – the love, with which this day and always you have surrounded us.'[6]

It was all the more moving, because this socially awkward sailor-king was not one to wear his heart on his sleeve. For twenty-five years, he had done his duty, gone through the motions of office. He and Queen Mary were, quite simply, adored by the British people, and by the people of the British Empire. His grand-daughter, who became Queen Elizabeth II, used to call him 'Grandfather England'. It was an appropriate nickname. He was an embodiment, and that is what a successful constitutional monarch can be. It is not yet possible to know how closely Elizabeth II has been involved with the political crises of her reign. For instance, what did she have to say to Tony Blair about the banishment of most hereditary peers from the House of Lords, and the failure of his Government to find a satisfactory way of selecting members of a Second Chamber. We know that George V was, willy nilly, involved in the Constitutional Crisis of 1909–11 – basically caused by the conflict between the strong Liberal Commons and the largely Conservative and Unionist Lords, who clashed over both Ireland and the Budget. The threat to create 500 Liberal peers to outvote the Tories in the Lords was one that George V rejected, but he was forced to accept the Parliament Bill, 1910, which made it impossible thereafter for the Lords to overturn fiscal decisions made by the Commons. (There had been cries of 'Traitor!' and 'Who Killed the King?' when the Liberal Prime Minister Herbert Asquith next appeared in the House of Commons.)[7]

In December 1910, Asquith sent a memo to George V that set out in no uncertain terms that the era of monarchical power was definitely over:

> The part to be played by the Crown... has happily been settled by the accumulated traditions and the unbroken practice of more than seventy years. It is to act upon the advice of Ministers who for the time being possess the confidence of the House of Commons, whether that advice does or does not conform to the private and personal judgement of the sovereign. Ministers will always pay the utmost deference, and give the most serious consideration, to any criticism or objection that the Monarch may offer to their policy; but the ultimate decision rests with them; for they, and not the Crown, are responsible to Parliament.[8]

At the other end of George V's reign when, the Liberal Party in tatters, the first Labour Government had been voted in, George, one of the most natural Tories imaginable, had been obliged to oversee the crisis caused by the financial collapse of 1934, and the choice facing the Labour Party – of voting to cut unemployment benefit or going bankrupt. The other parties expressed their willingness to serve in a National Government under Ramsay MacDonald, and this was the option favoured by King George. It destroyed MacDonald in the eyes of his party, and confirmed many Labour supporters in their republican instincts.

All this was to show that a constitutional monarch is not just a ceremonial figurehead. Though George V had no executive power, he did have a role, and it was one that history showed to have been that of a broker between differing political sects. He, for example, had chosen Baldwin as Conservative Prime Minister rather than Curzon, in 1923. He knew, however, that he must tread gently. Indeed, George V's obsession with the Russian Revolution was undying, and one of his great dreads, when there was a Labour Government in power, was that 'they', his Socialist ministers, would 'make' him shake hands with those who had murdered his relatives, that is, the new Soviet diplomats in London.

George V, who so terrified his sons, was also their political role model. It was the model which his son David – Edward VIII – was unable to follow, but the example of George V and Queen Mary was the tried and trusted role model for George VI and Queen Elizabeth, and for Queen Elizabeth II and Prince Philip, when their moments came.

From early childhood, Elizabeth – 'Lilibet' as she was known to her parents – had a close rapport with old King George V. Whereas others were terrified of the King's bad temper, she spoke to him with Cordelia-like directness. When he did a little drawing to amuse her, she responded, 'You really are not at all a bad drawer.'[9] When he fell ill, the doctors recommended her presence to heal him, and she was sent to Bognor Regis, where the King had a villa, to play on the sands, while he sat in a deck-chair on the seashore watching her. 'It was wonderful to see them together,' her governess recalled, 'the bearded old man and the polite little girl holding on to one of his fingers.'[10]

The decade of her birth was not a happy time to be a monarch. Just eight years before Elizabeth II was born, on 21 April 1926, her cousin the Emperor of Russia, his wife and his five teenage children, two servants and the family doctor were taken to a cellar in Ekaterinburg by Bolshevik revolutionaries, and done to death with revolvers and bayonets. In the same year, her cousin the German Emperor, Wilhelm II – in whose loving arms his grandmother Queen Victoria had died on the Isle of Wight in 1901 – abdicated the German throne, and went into exile in The Netherlands, where he lived until his death in 1941. There had been loud cries in Britain to have him hanged as a war criminal. In the same year as Wilhelm's Abdication, the last Emperor of Austria, the saintly Karl, was deposed. Even as Elizabeth was being born, Britain was in the grip of the General Strike, in which the middle and upper classes feared that the working classes would, unless robustly opposed, impose Communism in the United Kingdom. They were heady, miserable, times. The poor were really poor – unimaginably poor by the standards of early twenty-first-century Europe. Children in London had rickets, and lived on starvation rations.

The last years of the Russian monarchy had been a tragic melodrama. The Austro-Hungarian Empire, which was in some respects the surviving remnant of the Holy Roman Empire itself, was the *ancien régime* embodied in the figurehead of its Emperors, whose latter days had been marked, as had their Russian counterparts, by the excitement of assassination attempts and political extremism. The Wilhelmine regime in Germany was likewise technicoloured and dramatic.

The comparative boringness of the British court was an essential part of the success story of constitutional monarchy. That is why I began by emphasizing it. The dullness inspired Sir Max Beerbohm, that 1890s wit who lived out of time in the twentieth century, to write his famous 'Ballade Tragique à Double Refrain':

SCENE: A Room in Windsor Castle.

TIME: The Present

Enter a Lady-in-Waiting and a Lord-in-Waiting

SHE: Slow pass the hours—ah, passing, slow!
        My doom is worse than anything
        Conceived by Edgar Allan Poe:
        The Queen is duller than the King.

HE: Lady, your mind is wandering;
        You babble what you do not mean.
        Remember, to your heartening,
        The King is duller than the Queen.

SHE: No, most emphatically No!
        To one firm-rooted fact I cling
        In my now chronic vertigo:
        The Queen is duller than the King.

HE: Lady, you lie. Last evening
        I found him with a Rural Dean,
        Talking of district-visiting...
        The King is duller than the Queen.

SHE: At any rate he doesn't sew!
          You don't see him embellishing
          Yard after yard of calico...
          The Queen is duller than the King.
          Oh to have been an underling
          To (say) the Empress Josephine!

HE: Enough of your self-pitying!
          The King is duller than the Queen.

SHE   *(firmly)*: The Queen is duller than the King.

HE: Death then for you shall have no sting.

[*Stabs her and, as she falls dead, produces phial
from breast-pocket of coat.*]

    Nevertheless, sweet friend Strychnine,

[*Drinks.*]

    The King—is—duller than—the Queen.

[*Dies in terrible agony.*][11]

The British believe there is an old Chinese curse – 'May you live in interesting times.' Although the curse seems to be about as 'Chinese' as spring rolls manufactured for a Western supermarket, and no oriental original has ever been found for the saying, it is nonetheless a saying that applies to the monarchs of early twentieth-century Europe, and to the countries over which they once ruled. Nicholas II ruled over a very interesting court – rivetingly interesting when compared with the quiet routines of George V, sticking in his stamps of an evening while his wife did her embroidery. The Russian court was dominated by the wild-eyed peasant con-man and sex-maniac Rasputin, whom the Emperor and his wife pathetically believed could hold at bay, or even cure, the haemophilia by which their son was afflicted.

The Austrian and the German Empires were comparably 'interesting', and the destiny of all three Empires, once they had lost their monarchs, became 'interesting' to a nightmarish degree. Russia was plunged into the bloodiest of civil wars, in which the Bolsheviks were victorious. There followed the tyrannies of Lenin and Stalin, the establishment of the Gulag Archipelago, and an Eastern Europe, under the sway of Stalin, in which a huge proportion of the population were imprisoned, while the rest feared that their very thoughts might land them in prison or, worse, lead them to the firing-squad. This was to be the fate not only of the peoples of the former Russian Empire, but also of those lands from the former Austro-Hungarian Empire – Czechoslovakia, Hungary, the Balkan lands of Yugoslavia, Romania, Bulgaria – that had fallen under Stalin's sway or Stalin's threats. Meanwhile, the lands once controlled by the Prussian autocracy would, once the Emperor had abdicated, become briefly a Communist republic, and then a liberal-leftist republic (the Weimar years), eventually crippled by the international economic situation and overwhelmed by the rise of National Socialism. As the world watched the torch-lit processions and stupendously orchestrated rallies of the Third Reich, and noted the slow incremental growth of anti-Semitic legislation, it tried to block its ears to those who warned that Germany was rearming and preparing for war. Listening to Hitler's theatrical displays of rhetoric must have been a good way of making many British people feel thankful for the 'dullness' of their King and Queen and of their nebulous, unwritten Constitution.

Because the role of the monarchy in British political life had become so comparatively subdued in the era of our Queen's childhood, it was easy to believe that it actually played no significant part in keeping the country safe from the extremes which were destroying the lives of so many millions in Europe. It was easy to say that Britain did not have a Stalin or a Hitler because it had held fast to the institution of Parliament, because its laws were, comparatively speaking, more decent, its economy comparatively speaking more stable than those of Weimar Germany, Nazi Germany or the Stalinist East. No doubt there is much to be said for this point of view. Deeper and longer reflection, however, suggests that the monarchs themselves – George V, George VI and Elizabeth II – did play some role in maintaining the political stability of the nation. Precisely because this role was subdued, gentle, partial, it is difficult to quantify or to prove. Perhaps it is only as Elizabeth II's reign moves towards its close that we can begin to sense what we owe to these three monarchs who either dared to be dull or who had the good fortune to be born dull.

It was one thing to be dull. What, though, was the British monarch's function? Was George V doing anything that could not have been done equally efficiently by an elected President? Was there any need for the British to continue with their monarchy at all? For the first ten years of Lilibet's life, 'Grandfather England', when not killing animals or sticking in stamps, continued the patient, steady business of being a constitutional monarch. In one of his earliest audiences with Ramsay MacDonald, the King assured the Labour Leader that the sovereign does not discuss business with anyone other than his Private Secretary.[12] Whereas the treatment meted out to the King by the Liberals, and especially by Lloyd George, had 'bordered on the contemptuous',[13]

MacDonald 'kept him better informed than any of his predecessors had done'.[14] This pattern strangely enough was followed by later Labour leaders, James Callaghan, for example, noting the Queen's interest in the day-to-day ups and downs of politics. Yet there was no sense in which the monarch had his hand on the tiller of power. The Asquith–Lloyd George government had seen to that definitively and forever.

What remained to be seen, as George V's reign came to an end, was whether the old order could be maintained when his raffish bachelor son, Edward VIII – Lilibet's 'Uncle David' – came to the throne. When old King George eventually died, a young poet, John Betjeman, wrote one of the finest royal elegies in the English language. He imagined old men of the King's generation receiving the news – 'old men who never cheated, never doubted'[15] – and staring nervously towards the future world. Betjeman, in a sense, was seeing the same truth that had so amused Max Beerbohm. If you were writing a textbook on the Constitution, the power and function of the monarchy, you would say that the power and function of the monarchy, by 1936, had shrunk to almost nothing. Yet this was patently not the case, for, although politicians could carry on the business of government without the King, and treat him on occasion with contempt, there was another country which was definitely in touch with its monarch. That was the population of Great Britain, and its Empire, outside the Whitehall establishment. In 1936 Betjeman demonstrated that the monarchy and the British people enjoyed a symbiotic relationship which could perhaps only be defined in poetry. The extreme conservatism of 'Grandfather England' prompted many, not least his heir, to believe that the monarchy had to change in order to survive. Whether it would survive the arrival of Edward VIII remained only to be seen.

> Old men who never cheated, never doubted,
> Communicated monthly, sit and stare
> At the red suburb, stretched beyond the run-way
> Where a young man lands hatless from the air.

This was Lilibet's Uncle David. The delicate destiny of the British crown now lay in this rather stupid man's reckless hands.

2

'I SERVE'

'My whole life, whether it be long or short,
shall be devoted to your service'

PRINCESS ELIZABETH IN HER TWENTY-FIRST
BIRTHDAY BROADCAST

In 1965, the year that Churchill died, the 1930s had begun to seem a very long way away. The Queen's family, led by her mother, had behaved for nearly thirty years as if the exiled King, now the Duke of Windsor, did not exist. It was Queen Elizabeth II who decided to bring this state of affairs to an end. When the poor 'little Dook', as his friends in Paris called him, came over to the London Clinic for treatment on a detached retina, Lilibet went to visit her uncle. She spent about half an hour talking to him, bandaged and pyjama-clad, and to the stringy old Duchess Wallis. It was a sign that she had buried the hatchet. Some journalists claimed that when she left the hospital, the Queen was wiping a tear from her eye. During two or three days of convalescence, the pair were seen, uncle and niece, walking together in the gardens of Buckingham Palace.[16] She made another visit to see him in Paris when he was dying in 1971. By then, he weighed six stone. It had taken the nurses several hours to prepare him, getting him out of bed, removing the tubes, and dressing him in a blazer and trousers. Although he was on a carefully concealed drip, he rose to his feet to kiss her and to greet her as 'my dear'. She asked him how he was. 'Not so bad', was the reply in his strange voice, a mixture of his father's cockney and his wife's American. He was dead ten days later.[17]

Elizabeth's Uncle David reigned as King Edward VIII for less than a year. He inherited the crown on 20 January 1936, and he abdicated on 11 December. It was the shortest reign of a British monarch since that of his namesake, Edward V, one of the murdered 'Princes in the Tower'. Although his motto as Prince of Wales had been 'I serve', he had evidently resented any expectations that he would perform public duties unless he happened to feel like doing so. 'I did a bloody good job for my country, and all I got was a good kick in the ass,' was his own rather strange view of those bachelor years, whose daylight hours had been spent so often on golf courses and whose evenings were usually passed in nightclubs with married women.[18]

'Uncle David' had, as everyone knows, married for love, and chosen to defy the Canon Law of the Church of England – of which he was the Supreme Governor – by marrying a woman, Wallis Warfield, who had been twice divorced. 'You must believe me when I tell you that I have found it impossible to carry the heavy burden of responsibility and to discharge my duties as king as I would wish to do without the help and support of the woman I love.' So he had said in the wireless broadcast which immediately followed the Abdication.

The historian Ben Pimlott wrote that, in the short term, British politics were hardly affected by the Abdication and that it could be argued that the crisis had very little impact. Clearly, however, for Edward VIII's brother, who now inherited the throne as George VI, the Abdication had an enormous impact. The strain upon this shy naval officer, who was hampered by the most extreme stammer, was crippling; and it is not surprising that those close to him believed that the 'heavy burden of responsibility' hastened his death, at the age of fifty-six. When Harold Nicolson visited Queen Mary in 1949, she told him that George VI 'had been appalled when he succeeded. He was devoted to his brother and the whole Abdication crisis made him miserable. He sobbed on my shoulder for a whole hour – there, upon that sofa. Even his stammer had been corrected. And now he is so ill, poor boy, so ill.'[19]

The Abdication loomed over Lilibet's life and reign like a threatened curse. Her own parents had been such dutiful and successful monarchs. But the Abdication had shown what happened when a monarch broke the rules. Then, everything unravelled.

Had her Uncle David chosen a young, previously unmarried bride of child-bearing age, Elizabeth and Margaret Rose could have lived the comfortable lives of minor royalties, carrying out their duty, no doubt, but without the heaviness of 'the burden'. Had she married the same person, Prince Philip of Greece, he would have been able to pursue his career as a reasonably successful naval officer while his wife, no doubt, would have spent much of her time in the country with horses and dogs. His fellow officers could have guffawed at his supposedly humorous remarks, and they would never have been treasured by journalists in search of 'gaffes'.

As it was, the Church, and the Establishment, decreed that the King could not plausibly remain in position. The Christian abhorrence of divorce, and, in particular, of the remarriage of the divorced, was Edward VIII's undoing. In 1936 divorce was relatively unusual in Britain, and, whether people were Christian or not, they tended to avoid the divorce courts. In the

Royal Family, however, the spectre of Mrs Simpson's divorces would hover like a death's head over them.

Speaking of his brother Bertie, Edward VIII had said, in his Abdication broadcast, 'He has one matchless blessing, enjoyed by so many of you, and not bestowed on me – a happy home with his wife and children.' And this was true. For much of Elizabeth's reign, at the top of the stairs as one entered the National Portrait Gallery, there hung a painting by Sir James Gunn of King George VI, Queen Elizabeth and their two daughters having tea at Windsor. It is a scene of calm happiness, of domestic virtue, an emblem of all that the Nation escaped by not having the wise-cracking, chic, 'fast', thrice-married Wallis as their Queen. When, in 1955, Princess Margaret broke off her affair with Group-Captain Peter Townsend, who had been divorced, she did so 'mindful of the Church's teachings that Christian marriage is indissoluble, and conscious of my duty to the Commonwealth'.[20] Yet her own marriage to the photographer Antony Armstrong-Jones would come unstuck, as would the marriage of the Queen's eldest three children.

In 1933, when Elizabeth was just six and Margaret Rose two, her parents had engaged a young Scottish woman,

Marion Crawford – 'Crawfie' – as their governess. Their homes at this time were Royal Lodge in Windsor Great Park and 145 Piccadilly. The Duke and Duchess of York lived simply, seldom giving dinner parties. The four – the Yorks and the 'little princesses' – were close. It so happened that on the day after the Abdication, a friend of theirs, Lady Cynthia Asquith, was coming to tea. When she left 145 Piccadilly, Lilibet escorted her to the front door. She saw an envelope on the hall table addressed to 'Her Majesty the Queen'. With a tremor in her voice, Lilibet said, 'That's Mummie[21] now.'

The child was aware, everyone was aware – assuming the monarchy had a future at all – that she was next in line to the throne, that Lilibet would one day be the British Head of State. Even before this, Crawfie – and old Queen Mary – had expressed anxiety about the low level of education which was being offered to the little girls.[22] Queen Mary, who was a cultivated woman, bilingual in German and English, knowledgeable about ceramics and furniture, had mixed from her earliest youth with European royalties and nobility, and saw at first hand the apparent deliberation with which the British Royal Family failed to educate their children. When she met her husband's biographer, Harold Nicolson, she complained about the inadequacy of his tutor, Canon Dalton. 'It was disgraceful that "the King" had not been taught more.

I asked whether he could speak French really well. She did not like that question. "No," she said rather stiffly.'[23]

Lilibet's parents, however, despite Queen Mary's urgings, continued to educate her and her sister rather as the daughters of an Earl of Strathmore might have been educated in Edwardian or late Victorian times. At least, unlike King George V, they both spoke French beautifully – Elizabeth's French, in particular, is fluent and bell-like, with an English accent which is charming rather than being absurd. It is true that, from 1938 onwards, when she was in Windsor, Princess Elizabeth was sent to be taught constitutional history by the Provost of Eton, Sir Henry Marten. He thought highly of Princess Elizabeth's capabilities – and saw 'great stuff' in her. As well as explaining the Constitution, he gave her a comprehensive course on the explorers, starting with Columbus, and ending with the present day, pointing out the new territories in an atlas. He also told her the history of the United States, pacing up and down his room, and occasionally turning to ask, 'Is that clear to you, gentlemen?'[24] It was not much, however, when one considers how relatively soon she would become Head of State and Head of what was no longer an Empire, but remained a Commonwealth of nations. The Abdication crisis could easily have destroyed the monarchy itself. Carrying forward the monarchy into an unknown future was an immense responsibility.

Throughout Elizabeth's reign, criticism was levelled against her parents for their apparently irresponsible attitude, and against the Queen herself for not being better educated. The historian Dr David Starkey, for example, who had accepted a 'gong' from the Queen – he is a Commander of the British Empire – felt the need to preserve his reputation as 'the rudest man in Britain', after he had curated an exhibition about Queen Elizabeth I in Greenwich in 2003. The exhibition was opened by the sovereign, and she did not impress the historian.

'I think she's got elements a bit like Goebbels in her attitude to culture,' the historian told the *Guardian*. 'You remember: "Every time I hear the word culture I reach for my revolver."'

He found her 'more preoccupied with the late arrival of her drink (gin and Dubonnet) than the works on display. Her only comment on the exhibition was that one of the objects was hers'.

This, said Starkey, reminded him of 'a housewife' who'd been left some wonderful possessions. 'She's looked after them, she's put in place much better arrangements for their care, but again – I suppose it's this absence of any kind of – to be blunt – serious education.'

He could not help comparing her with Elizabeth I, who also acceded the throne at twenty-five, 'but was twenty times as well educated. And had either five or six languages.'

He was also struck that the Queen does not seem to have any interest in those who preceded her grandfather, George V.

Starkey said that he had read all of her Christmas broadcasts. 'It's quite fascinating, because her frames of reference to the monarchy, despite this 1,500-year history, are entirely her father and grandfather... There is a reference to Elizabeth I. It was in the second Christmas broadcast when – I remember vividly – there was all this talk about a second Elizabethan age. Elizabeth turns to this in her broadcast, and says: "Frankly, I do not myself feel at all like my Tudor forebear, who was blessed with neither husband nor children, who ruled as a despot and was never able to leave her native shores."'[25]

Ours is a generation whose belief in formal education, by which we mean schooling and universities, has reached the level of a superstition, that is, an irrational belief which cannot be questioned. Even to question it would be, to opinion-formers, civil servants or politicians, all of whom have been through the education-mill, a kind of madness. They assume that the only way in which a person can be adequately suited for life is by what Tony Blair, before becoming Prime Minister, called 'education, education, education'. (Three excellent reasons for distrusting him.)

In relatively recent times, however, Britain was largely inhabited by people whom Dr Starkey and Tony Blair would regard as 'uneducated', but who were in fact perfectly competent in their chosen spheres. Today, it is regarded as shocking in many quarters, for example, that some nurses do not possess degrees; and it is even said that such nurses are not 'qualified'. In the past, however, nurses learnt from experience, 'on the job'. This was true of almost all walks of life – from young barristers in chambers, to bankers, to shopkeepers, to artisans who passed through apprenticeships, to those who worked, at whatever level, in agriculture. Universities catered, not for the 'upper classes', who – except in a tiny number of cases throughout history – scarcely went near them – but for that much smaller category, the genuinely scholarly. During the nineteenth century, they had also been seen as useful training grounds for diplomats and civil servants. The great majority of British people, however, during all the years when Britain was most successful, either as an economy or as a world power, achieved their success without the formality of 'education'. The Queen, when it came to it, like most of her subjects – farmers, motor mechanics, plumbers, solicitors, parish clergy – would learn 'on the job'.

One footnote to Dr Starkey. It is a mistake always to assume, as he evidently does, that limitations are always a disadvantage in life. The history don was dismayed that 'the Queen does not seem to have any interest in those who preceded her grandfather, George V'.[26] No doubt, if the Queen had been applying for a place as a mature student at university to study British history, this would be a serious handicap. Given her role in life, however, there is a certain aptness in her looking back no further than to 'Grandfather England'. For it was with him that, in effect, her story began. Not only was he the King when she was born. He was her role model. He had redefined what it meant to be a constitutional monarch in what was, for most of Europe, a post-monarchical age. For this reason, Elizabeth did not need to look back further than to him, when she was learning her 'trade'. When so many hereditary monarchies, all over Europe, had toppled, during the decade which preceded Elizabeth's birth, the British one had remained. It did so by the delicate balancing act of, on the one hand, remaining 'the same', and on the other, adapting. One obvious example of this was the alacrity with which George V took to making a broadcast Christmas message on the newly invented wireless. His reclusive grandmother, Queen Victoria, even assuming that the wireless had been invented in her day, would never have been persuaded to make a broadcast. For her, the constitutional monarch was an essentially aloof figure – she would not even read the 'Queen's Speech' at the State Opening of Parliament – it was read for her by the Lord Chancellor. 'Grandfather England' was, by the end of his reign, a popular figure, and the willingness to engage with the most up-to-date media was one of the reasons for this. He had sensed the PR value of broadcasting.

No one, when Elizabeth was a young child, could have foreseen quite how much 'image' and 'presentation' would mean in the unfolding decades. Had they done so, perhaps some attention would have been given to the way in which Princess Elizabeth and her sister were taught to speak the English language. Or then again (given the character of her mother), perhaps not. The Duchess of York was a strong-minded, jolly woman who would have mocked any idea of teaching her children a more demotic way of pronouncing words. The Queen's mother spoke an English which was a throwback to country houses pre-1914; her upper class voice was of a particularly uncompromising timbre; though both her daughters were less high-pitched than their mother, it was this voice, rather than that of their father's, which they inherited. George VI, when he could get words out at all, had recognizably the 'royal cockney' twang of his father and brother, with perhaps a hint of the Royal Navy officer in his voice. Had Elizabeth II spoken like 'Grandfather England', her public image in the early years of her reign would undoubtedly have been different. In 1957, in an attempt to puncture some of the sycophancy and idolatry which the young Queen Elizabeth II was larded by the press, the young journalist-historian John Grigg (Lord Altrincham) described her voice as 'a pain in the neck', which gave the impression of 'a priggish schoolgirl, captain of the hockey team, a prefect and a recent candidate for Confirmation'.[27] Certainly, what neither her mother nor father, who lived cocooned in a very limited social sphere, could possibly have foreseen was the extent of social change which would come to Britain during and after the Second World War.

While Celia Johnson was having a smut removed from her eye by Trevor Howard in *Brief Encounter* ('Are you engry?', 'Not engry, just disappointed'), it was still possible for figures in public life to speak in the version of English classified by Nancy Mitford to be 'U'. By the time Harold Macmillan had become Prime Minister in 1956, it was becoming quaint. By the time Harold Wilson became Prime Minister in 1964, it was undoubtedly the fact that he spoke with a Yorkshire accent which helped to propel him to victory over the 14th Earl of Home

(Sir Alec Douglas-Home, as he became), who spoke with an Etonian drawl, interrupted by rather engaging giggles. Thereafter, those who spoke with even traces of 'posh' on radio or television sounded increasingly odd. What would have been 'Received Pronunciation' in 1950 sounded distinctly upper crust by 1980, and most politicians or figures in public life who have tried to sell their 'ordinariness' to the rest of us have done so by neutralizing their voices. (Tony Blair's glottal stops come to mind.) The Queen's voice has changed a little since she was crowned. When she says 'off' the vowel is some way closer to the way in which it is spelt than it was when she said the same word in 1950. But she still says 'heppy' for 'happy' and 'orphan' for 'often'. 'Coffee' rhymes with 'Crawfie'. Queen Victoria's house on the Isle of Wight is pronounced 'Uzb'n'. Much as it has been mocked, the voice is now so much part of the Queen that it is unimaginable to think of her speaking in any other way.

The voice might be a throwback to house parties in the era of L.P. Hartley's *The Go-Between*, where the past was another country. The Queen, however, did not grow up in country-house luxury; though her mother might have employed the equivalent of P.G. Wodehouse's Anatole the Chef for her celebratedly sybaritic widowhood, the Queen retained, as so many did who had lived through the Second World War, what must have amounted to an enjoyment of austerity. Someone who went for an interview at Balmoral in the late 1990s for a job as a minor official in the royal entourage was delighted to be invited for luncheon with his sovereign. No alcohol was offered, and the menu consisted of macaroni cheese with mashed potato.[28] During the war years – when a German bomber scored a direct hit on Buckingham Palace – the King and Queen insisted upon staying in London. When possible, they went to Windsor to see their daughters who were immured in the castle. A high point of the princesses' week was the egg which they were each allowed to consume on Sunday mornings – they ate it fried until lard became scarce.[29]

Lilibet was a serious child and adolescent, and, without being pompous, she was aware of herself, from an early age, as a being set apart. Some of the earliest bombs of the war fell on Windsor. During the first of the raids, alarm bells rang in the castle, and Miss Crawford, the governess, ran to the air-raid shelter where she met Sir Hill Child, Master of the Household. Where were the Princesses? They were in the nursery with Mrs Knight ('Allah'[30]), their old nurserymaid, who remained with Lilibet until her death from meningitis in 1946. (She had been the Queen Mother's nanny before that; 'Allah/ Alah' was a childish attempt to pronounce her first name, Clara.)

The governess ran to the nursery and said through the door, 'Alah, it's Crawfie. Lord Wigram [Deputy Constable and Lieutenant Governor of the Castle] and Sir Hill Child and everybody else is waiting in the shelter and you must come down. This is not a dress rehearsal. What are you doing?'

It was Lilibet's voice which came back through the door.

'We're dressing, Crawfie. We must dress.'[31]

The heir to the throne was not to be seen in her pyjamas. It is a moment which recalls the life of the first Queen Elizabeth, when the Earl of Essex precipitated his fall from grace by bursting in upon her first thing in the morning in her *déshabillé*.

The war against Hitler united Great Britain in a way that nothing had done before, and nothing has done since. There was a common enemy, and an enemy moreover who was obviously hateful, and who, equally obviously, had to be destroyed. At the key moment in the historical drama, 1940, it did not merely *look* as if Britain and its Empire stood alone against Hitler: it really was the case, and this had provided a heady sense of national pride, almost euphoria. The brave chain-smoking King, who had served as a naval officer, and spoke with such an appalling speech impediment, and his calm, radiant Queen were the perfect opposites to Hitler: the King, who seemed so ill, so pious and so modest, the polar opposite to Hitler's power mania; the Queen, who seemed like one of the jollier aunts in P.G. Wodehouse, being the opposite to Hitler's humourlessness. Hensley Henson, the Bishop of Durham, wrote in his diary, having heard the Christmas broadcast for 1944, 'I doubt if any of his predecessors, hardly excepting Queen Victoria, drew to the Throne so great a volume of affection and respect... and he owes much to the sweetness and steady persistence of Queen Elizabeth.'[32] Hensley Henson was not noted for his kind view of human nature. Nearly all his richly entertaining diary entries about public figures are magnificently phrased insults. The combination of the war and the peculiar charms of both King and Queen did indeed create a feeling of undiluted admiration. It was an admiration which brushed off on Lilibet, for whom there was also high love; and it was also an admiration which she shared. In 1945, aged nineteen, she volunteered to 'do her bit' and joined the Auxiliary Territorial Service as Number 230873 Second Subaltern Elizabeth Alexandra Mary Windsor. She learnt a lot about the internal combustion engine, and she perfected her driving skills. It was the first time a member of the

Royal Family had ever attended a course also attended by 'other people', and, although she was surrounded by minders, and she did not sleep in barracks at Camberley with the other women but was driven back each night to Windsor Castle, it was a taste of 'ordinary life'. On 27 July 1945, she was given the rank of junior commander. 'I've never worked so hard in my life,' she told a friend. 'Everything I learnt was brand new to me – all the oddities of the insides of a car, and all the intricacies of map-reading. But I enjoyed it all very much and found it a great experience.'[33]

Two years after the war, Elizabeth and Margaret Rose accompanied the King and Queen on a tour of South Africa. The journey had a number of purposes. One was Imperial. It was hoped that the King's arrival would strengthen the hand of Prime Minister Jan Smuts against the Nationalists in the forthcoming elections. In fact, the royal visit was powerless to stop the march of Boer Nationalism, and shortly after the King came back to England, the Apartheid system began.

From the perspective of the early twenty-first century, it is obvious that the British Empire was, in effect, finished by the time of the ending of the war. It was not obvious to many of the British ruling class, and it certainly was not obvious to the Royal Family. Mountbatten was being dispatched by the Labour Government, in 1947, as the last Viceroy of India, with the task of winding up the show without too great mishap. As we know, he bungled it spectacularly, with over a million killed after Partition. (One reason for his haste was his desire to be back in Britain to witness his nephew's wedding to Princess Elizabeth.)

Princess Elizabeth's preoccupation with Prince Philip was another reason for the royal party going to South Africa – George VI wanted his daughter to be quite sure that she wanted to marry him. She had met him first when she was just thirteen. He was a naval cadet, five years her senior. The King liked a fellow naval officer in the making. It would seem as if Lilibet had genuinely fallen for him, though, as Prince Philip himself was to put it, with his usual lack of tact, there were not many obvious suitors. 'After all, if you spend ten minutes thinking about it… how many obviously eligible young men, other than people living in this country, were available?'[34] Some months away from Philip, in the company of her parents, would give the Princess time to make up her mind.

Another, and more ominous, reason for the visit was that it was hoped that the winter sunshine of South Africa would soothe the King's very poor health.

It was while they were in South Africa that the Princess celebrated her twenty-first birthday, and made her broadcast to the Empire. It was written for her by Alan Lascelles – always known as 'Tommy' – the King's Private Secretary, and it was, as has been said many times, in effect a political broadcast on behalf of British Imperialists. It was intended to persuade the South Africans to retain their links with the Empire, and it was also meant to persuade the Indians, even after they had achieved independence, to maintain friendly relations with the British. In neither was it completely successful. As the inauguration of young Elizabeth on to the public stage, however, it achieved immortality. 'I declare before you all that my whole life, whether it be long or short, shall be devoted to your service and the service of our great Imperial family to which we all belong...'

They returned home that spring, 1947. It was clear to Elizabeth that as she began her life of public service, she would do so accompanied by Philip of Greece. The wedding was fixed for 20 November, in Westminster Abbey.

3

'CHEER UP, SAUSAGE'

'Where did you get that hat?'

PRINCE PHILIP TO THE QUEEN, AFTER THE CORONATION[35]

The Diamond Jubilee Celebrations in June 2012 were marked by a spectacular water procession. The Queen and the Duke of Edinburgh, in a splendid launch, were followed and accompanied down the Thames by a flotilla of vessels, which included some of the 'little boats' that had rescued servicemen from the beaches of Dunkirk in the summer of 1940, gondolas, cutters of the City Livery Companies – in short, symbols of various aspects of the Queen's realm and reign. The imaginative organizers, chaired by the Marquess of Salisbury, said that they had been inspired by the canvases of Canaletto, whose views, both of the Thames and of the Venetian lagoon, always present a calm scene of sunlit, blue water on which the boats glide like little toys.

The Queen, whose coronation was accompanied by torrential rainfall, is a rain goddess; so, it was no surprise that what had been conceived as a picture by Canaletto became something different. On one level, the pageant was all but ruined by the modern requirements of Security. Those of us who tried to watch from the bank were confronted by barriers and police and 'volunteers', blocking off almost every street. Even in wide open spaces, such as Battersea Park, people found it difficult to reach the water's edge. It was not only a wet day: it was very cold. Yet wherever you tried to evade the officious barricades and actually witness the water-spectacular, the same phenomenon was observable: a crowd which was almost desperate in its desire to cheer the monarch. Sodden Union Jacks were waved aloft with that ironical combination of humours – mockery, self-mockery, banter – which 'come over' British crowds when they are trying to hide from themselves a collective excitement, a palpable fervour. Nothing could be more different from the crowds at a North Korean or Nuremberg-style celebration of the Great Leader. The mood swooped between attempts not to 'well up' with grumbling about the weather and the police.

And there they were on the water – the Queen and Prince Philip: 'my husband and I'. For the two hours or so which it took the Royal Barge to make its journey, the monarch and her husband stood. Much was made of this at the time – as if they were being especially heroic. On one level, they were. On another level, they had little alternative, since the gales had swept over the launch for the few hours before the Queen took her place in it, and the seats provided for the royal party were sodden. They were faced with a choice of a dignified but exhausting few hours standing upright or the same length of time seated in deep, cold puddles. Not long afterwards, Prince Philip was taken off to hospital. Those of us who are sometimes invited by newspapers or the broadcast media to make comments on royal deaths were put on alert. We stood beside our laptops with black armbands to the ready. In fact, as so often before, and as several times since, it was a false alarm, and after a week in hospital, the seemingly indefatigable old man was soon back in action.

Few who saw it, however, will forget the sight of the Queen and Prince Philip standing for hours upon that rain-assaulted ceremonial vessel. On the one hand, there was near-absurdity in the sight. What had been planned so lovingly as a sun-blessed picture of eighteenth-century tranquillity had become an episode of the late Queen Mother's favourite television comedy show, *Dad's Army* – where such events as pageants and parades so often descended into farce. On the other hand, the unscheduled and unchoreographed need to make this pair of very old people stand for such a dangerously long time spoke more vividly than if they had drifted past us sitting comfortably on crimson velvet. There they stood. Short of death itself – which looked, towards the end of the day, as if it was on the point of carrying at least one of them away – nothing could apparently dislodge their dogged willingness to stand, and stand, and stand, as the cold wind blew, and the rains fell.

Prince Philip's ramrod uprightness as a supporter of the contemporary monarchy is not in question, any more than is his very distinctive character. During the celebrations for the seventy-fifth anniversary of the Battle of Britain, in July 2015, he found himself being made to pose for a photograph with a group of distinguished airmen, old and young. Most of them were in uniform. He was on this occasion in a blue lounge suit, his chest adorned with medals. He shares with his father-in-law and grandfather-in-law an obsession with decorations, medals, ceremonial uniforms and correct court rituals. By now, he had come to resemble the most distinguished old member of a seaside bowls club, with slightly alarming eyes starting furiously from his angular, though still handsome, skull. The photographer was dithering. Everyone was bored. At last came one of those moments which Prince Philip-watchers always treasure. 'Just take the fucking picture!' came his barking voice.

At a luncheon given to celebrate their Golden Wedding anniversary in 1997, the Queen said, 'He is someone who doesn't take easily to compliments, but he has, quite simply, been my strength and stay all these years, and I, and his whole family, in this and in many other countries, owe him a debt greater than he would ever claim or we shall ever know.'[36]

At the time of Philip and Elizabeth's betrothal, there had been misgivings. Tommy Lascelles probably spoke for the rest of the court when he said they all considered him to be 'rough, ill-mannered, uneducated, and would probably not be faithful'.[37] Both points of view were held with equal vigour throughout the long marriage. Both points of view were plausible. Probably, by now, some people are beginning to realize that one of the things which has enabled him to be the Queen's strength and stay for so long is that he has been at least some of the things which Tommy Lascelles and colleagues deplored. What the courtiers had viewed as defects were in fact assets in a marriage to a shy woman who, despite her clear goodness of heart, has seldom been able to convey interest in or affection for the people she meets.

On their very first major Commonwealth tour, in 1953, the Queen and Prince Philip found themselves in a little town in South Australia. The mayor, very nervous, and dressed in what were described as 'dreadful homemade robes of bunny rabbit fur', presented his monarch with a box. 'Your Royal Highness,' he blunderingly said, rather than 'Your Majesty', 'at this very moment, our High Commissioner in London is presenting a similar box to your representative at the Palace.' 'Oh, my God, man!' roared Prince Philip. 'Don't you realize the ten-and-a-half-hour time difference between here and England? The High Commissioner is probably sound asleep at this minute!'[38]

Of course, it was cruel. Nonetheless, it is also funny. And there were several occasions during that tour when the Queen, going through the motions and doing her duty, could not rise to do any more than her duty, whereas he remained a recognizably human being. When the temperatures in Australia soared to 110°F and the Queen, pining for the cold air and damp heather of Balmoral, could not remove the scowl from her face, he said, 'Cheer up, sausage, it's not so bad as all that.' Later, in New Zealand, when they were greeted by a crowd of Maori children jumping up and down on a riverbank, the Queen did not even cast them a glance. It was Philip who called out, 'Look, Bet, aren't they lovely?'[39] ('Bet' is short for Lilibet; this is what he calls her.)

Journalists, and many of their readers, so enjoy Prince Philip's 'gaffes' that they sometimes make them up, as when, during the 1990s, he attended a pop concert in Wales with some deaf children, and was supposed to have said, 'No wonder you're deaf, having to listen to this racket!' (That was one of the few occasions when he was pompous enough to write a correction, pointing out that his own mother had suffered acutely from her deafness, and he would never have mocked the affliction.) The parodist who invented the comment had, however, caught the tone of the remarks which genuinely are authentic. To a group of women at a community centre in London's East End a few years ago, 'Who do you sponge off?' To the President of Nigeria who was wearing his national costume, 'You look like you're ready for bed.' To a tourist in Budapest, 'You can't have been here long, you haven't got a pot belly.' To a British trekker in Papua New Guinea, 'You managed not to get eaten, then?' To a civil servant in the 1970s, 'You're just a silly little Whitehall twit. You don't like me and I don't like you.' To a female naval rating in 2015, 'Do you work in a strip club?'

To a man who told him that he worked at the Samaritans, 'Ah, the Samaritans. You didn't try to commit suicide, did you?'

The Queen was bending over a man injured by an IRA bomb, who had lost much of his sight. 'How much can you see?' she inquired. 'Not a lot,' said the Duke, 'judging by that tie he's wearing.'[40]

To the matron of a Caribbean hospital, 'You have mosquitos. I have the press.' Seeing a press photographer fall out of a tree in Pakistan, 'I hope to God he breaks his bloody neck.'[41]

Prince Philip's relationship with the press has been abrasive, but humorous. During the first world tour he made with the Queen in 1953, he threw peanuts at the journalists awaiting them at Gibraltar near the ape enclosure. 'Which ones are the monkeys?' he asked them.[42]

At the same time, as he must have come to realize as he moved from the ripeness of old age to his tenth decade, he had enjoyed a remarkably easy ride with the press, compared with any of his children. From the 1950s onwards there were rumours about the marriage. He took risks. For many years, he drove himself round London in a black taxi-cab. Sometimes he would use this conveyance to take chums to bars or nightspots in Soho. They were never photographed, and their visits to such haunts were never reported. The rumours about his close relationships with a string of women were never substantiated, and there were those, such as Gyles Brandreth who wrote a broadly sympathetic book entitled *Philip and Elizabeth: Portrait of a Marriage*, who evidently came to believe that the relationships, however close, were all Platonic. Brandreth concluded his book (which is much the best I have read on the subject, partly because he does actually know Prince Philip), 'And how about the Queen? How does she feel about all this in the dark watches of the night? She cannot say, fully, freely, as Robert Browning says in his poem, "By the Fireside", "We stood there with never a third". But Robert Browning was a sentimentalist, which the Queen is not. She knows her man, loves him, admires him and accepts him as he is. She is also Sovereign of the Order of the Garter. *Honi soit qui mal y pense.*'[43]

Prince Philip has certainly been part of the success story of the twentieth-century British monarchy. No doubt there could have been other ways of making it a success, but his combination of abrasiveness and constancy has worked. He has been a dutiful servant of the state, both as a young naval officer, and as a friend and encourager of serving members of the armed forces. When he was eighty-five, two days after a whirlwind tour of the Baltic states with the Queen, the Duke of Edinburgh flew out to Basra to make a surprise visit to the Queen's Royal Hussars (of which he is Colonel in Chief). He was dressed in combat gear, and the visit could not have been better-judged. He was a man among men – a role which he can always fulfil cheerfully.

Lance Corporal Dean Munn, aged twenty-two from Redditch, remarked, 'it's good to see him here in these hard conditions, taking the time to see us and how we're doing'.[44] Eight years later, when he was ninety-three, this time wearing a bowler hat and 'civvies', the Prince flew to Sennelager, in Germany, to welcome back a hundred men of the tank regiment of the Queen's Royal Hussars and to pin Afghanistan medals on their chests. By now skeletally thin, with eyes which sparkled from the depths of his skull in the way that lights up the faces of those in the last stages of life, he was in jovial form. The off-colour jokes and laddish behaviour with women which had supposedly clouded earlier decades of his life would only have enhanced his standing with these men.

Many of those who have known Prince Philip personally have commented upon his sensitivity, which is a quality which plainly exists side by side with the abrasiveness.

Gyles Brandreth wrote, 'in May 1999, talking to the Duke about Diana, I said to him, "The public view of you, for what it is worth, is of a grouchy old man, unsympathetic to his daughter-in-law but I happen to know, not from you, but I know it, that when things were difficult, you wrote to Diana – kind letters, concerned, fatherly, caring letters from pa, explaining how you knew, first hand, the difficulties involved in marrying into the royal family". He smiled at me. "The impression the public has got is unfair," I said. He shrugged, "I've just got to live with it," he said.'[45]

Those who wish to know about Prince Philip's extraordinary upbringing are recommended to read Hugo Vickers's biography of the Prince's mother, *Alice, Princess Andrew of Greece* (2000), a book written with the Prince's full permission. Prince Philip's parents were, to put it mildly, ill-matched. His father was an impoverished royal playboy who ran away from marriage with a woman who suffered from severe mental illness. Alice's delusions took lurid form, and before being incarcerated in Dr Ludwig Binswanger's sanatorium in Switzerland, she had revealed her belief that she had had a carnal relationship with Christ.

In 1937 the family underwent an appalling tragedy when a plane-load of their relations flew to London from Darmstadt for a wedding. Flying in dense fog, the plane hit a chimney over a brickworks near Ostend and burst into flames. In one instant, the bridegroom, Ludwig of Hesse-Darmstadt, had lost almost his entire family, including Prince Philip's sister Cecile, aged twenty-six, and her two boys, Ludwig (six) and Alexander (four), who were to have been pages at the wedding of their Uncle

Ludwig to Margaret Geddes. Prince Philip was told of the tragedy while he was at school at Gordonstoun and never forgot the 'profound shock'.[46] The dreadful funeral took place in Germany, attended by Philip's three surviving sisters and their husbands. Kaiser Wilhelm II in his Dutch exile sent a representative; Reichsmarschall Göring was there in person.

One of the strange consequences of the tragedy was that Alice in her heartbreak recovered her wits. When war broke out, she insisted on returning to Athens, where she lived in a flat, chain-smoking and praying, accompanied by her cats and, more heroically on her part, by the family of a Jewish property developer named Haimaki Cohen. At great risk to herself, she concealed their existence from the Gestapo, and saved their lives. She never spoke of this episode and it only came to light when Freddy Cohen, one of Haimaki's sons, told friends after the war, and the story emerged in Basil Boothroyd's biography of Prince Philip. In her later years, living at Buckingham Palace, Alice dressed as a nun, and was fervent in her Greek Orthodox piety. She was buried on the Mount of Olives in the Russian Orthodox convent, and in April 1993 she was given a posthumous award in Israel as one who had been 'Righteous Among the Nations'. Prince Philip, in a skull-cap, collected the medal at Yad Vashem, the Holocaust remembrance centre in Jerusalem.[47]

Prince Philip's childhood and early life were, therefore, troubled, and he learnt early on to deal with disaster by breeziness. To Hugo Vickers, his mother's biographer, he said, 'I was at school in England and suddenly my family had gone. My father was in the South of France and my mother was just ill. I had to get on with it.'[48]

A key figure in Prince Philip's upbringing, as in that of Prince Charles, was the brother of Princess Alice, Prince Louis – 'Uncle Dickie' – known as Lord Mountbatten. The Battenbergs – poor relations of the Hesse-Darmstadts, into whose family Queen Victoria had married her daughter Princess Alice – were renamed the Mountbattens at the time of the First World War. Philip's grandfather had been the First Sea Lord who on 4 August 1914 had sent the signal: 'Admiralty to All Ships. Commence hostilities against Germany.'[49] But he had always spoken with a German accent, and he was, as a bargain-basement German princeling in charge of the British Navy, in an impossible position. He resigned as First Sea Lord and became Lord Milford Haven. The King himself, George V, whose family had been known as Saxe-Coburg-Gotha, renamed the Royal Family the

Windsors, prompting one of the German Emperor's better jokes: 'Now, I suppose, we shall have performances of the *Merry Wives of Saxe-Coburg*'.

Philip's background, therefore, as a young naval officer with no money when he had married Princess Elizabeth, had been uncertain. No wonder he had seemed to some observers to be over-assertive, not to say bullying, in his demeanour towards her.

Lord Mountbatten had achieved his kingmaking ambition. The Battenbergs, who, two generations earlier, had been almost derisory 'poor relations', were now to father the future Kings and Queens of England.

What were they to be called? Philip's surname, when he was Prince Philip of Greece, was Schleswig-Holstein-Sonderburg-Glücksburg. The British Royal Family could scarcely be expected to adopt this mouthful as its totally inappropriate name. When he became a naturalized British subject, he did so simply as Lieutenant Philip Mountbatten. There was talk, both at the time of his marriage and at the time of Prince Charles's birth, of the children adopting the surname Mountbatten, but this was hotly contested, by Queen Mary, by the court, and by the Cabinet, prompting Prince Philip, in his fury, to exclaim that he was regarded as nothing but a 'bloody AMOEBA'.[50] By 1960, when Prince Andrew was born, the issue was raised once more. The Lord Chancellor proposed that the dynastic name of the family remained Windsor, but the name of any 'deroyalized' grandson etc. of the Queen and Prince Philip could be 'Mountbatten-Windsor'. It seemed as if the Queen had no desire to change the family name, and that this impulse came from her husband, and, of course, the irrepressible 'Uncle Dickie'.

When Harold Macmillan visited Sandringham in 1960, after Christmas, he bumped into the Duke of Gloucester, the Queen's uncle, 'greatly disturbed'. 'Thank goodness you've come, Prime Minister. The Queen's in a terrible state; there's a fellow called Jones in the billiard room who wants to marry her sister, and Prince Philip's in the library wanting to change the family name to Mountbatten.'[51] One source close to the Royal Family said it was the only occasion he had seen the Queen in tears.

The trivial matter of a surname, like the royal obsession with orders, medals and decorations, was a sign, of course, that they had no power. By the end of the reign, no one probably minds what surname is adopted by the Queen's grandchildren. When people think of the Duke of Edinburgh, they do not think of him as an amoeba. They remember his jokes, and they recall that unbending faithful public servant standing in his uniform, upright in the rain.

4

DEFENDER OF THE FAITH

'I die a Christian according to the profession of the Church of England, as I found it left me by my father.'
CHARLES I ON THE SCAFFOLD, 30 JANUARY 1649

The most richly enjoyable biography of any modern Archbishop of Canterbury must be Humphrey Carpenter's *Robert Runcie: The Reluctant Archbishop*. Carpenter was a man of stupendous charm. His father was Bishop of Oxford, who lived in the village of Cuddesdon, just outside Oxford. Bob Runcie, during Carpenter's boyhood, was Principal of the theological college which was just over the road from the Bishop's Palace. So, the two men were good friends. Both were ebullient and amusing gossips, who could keep any table in a roar with indiscreet talk. Both were highly intelligent. When it was suggested that Humphrey Carpenter should be Runcie's biographer, the retired Archbishop agreed with alacrity.

What Carpenter did was to tape-record hours and hours of Runcie's conversation. Unlike many Archbishops, Runcie was a man of the world. He had served with distinction in the 3rd Battalion of the Scots Guards, and fought on the Normandy beaches in 1944. He had a wide social circle, and he was not in the least parsonical. 'I got the same story from everyone,' Carpenter wrote, 'that he was charming, witty, a good mimic, and had an eye for the girls; and that no one would have guessed he would land up in the church.'[52] Land up, however, he did, and he was a popular, and indeed distinguished, Archbishop of Canterbury. As someone who had been in the Oxford University Conservatives with Margaret Roberts, he was well qualified to stand up to her when he had become Archbishop and she was Prime Minister Thatcher. The pair differed sharply over social questions (the excellent paper *Faith in the City* appeared under his watch, a document arguing for better investment in Britain's inner cities, but which Thatcher regarded as Communist). He it was who conducted the Service of Thanksgiving in St Paul's Cathedral to celebrate the British victory in the Falkland Islands, and insisted upon remembering – much to Thatcher's near-apoplectic rage – the Argentinians who had been killed. The woman who had spent the Second World War selling pudding-rice and cheap tea to the good people of Grantham felt entitled to regard the Guards Officer Runcie as a 'wet'.

Needless to say, Runcie spoke wittily, fascinatingly and indiscreetly into Carpenter's tape recorder, upon all manner of subjects. This was the man who had married Prince Charles to Lady Diana Spencer and said in his sermon, 'here is the stuff of which fairy tales are made'. This was the man who spoke at the eightieth birthday of Elizabeth the Queen Mother at St Paul's: 'She has occupied the centre of the stage since 1923 without suffering the fate which so frequently befalls the fashionable personality who is played out after 10 years or so in the public eye'.[53]

After Humphrey Carpenter's book appeared, there were howls of protest, loudest of all from Runcie's wife Lindy, but also from the Archbishop himself. He claimed that Carpenter had broken some confidentiality agreement and that he should not have quoted so much of his talk. Since it had all been recorded he could scarcely claim that he was being quoted 'out of context', but the whole thing made a fascinating episode. Now that the years have passed – Carpenter himself died very young, in 2005, and Runcie has been dead since 2000 – it is possible to wonder whether Runcie did not on some level intend his words to have a wider currency. True, Carpenter betrayed Runcie's trust by printing bits of their conversations which the Archbishop would prefer to have kept secret. On the other hand, Runcie had known his biographer from childhood onwards, and he knew that Carpenter was scarcely a by-word for discretion.

In particular, Runcie had been embarrassed by the publication of his thoughts about Prince Charles and Diana. Clearly, he had been in a position of trust with the pair, and he revealed that, when the marriage was becoming rocky, Charles had asked Runcie to have a chat with Diana. As Runcie happily blabbed, 'Diana felt she had a special relationship with me, because I took her brother Charlie's wedding, and baptised his children as well as hers. And I became and remain a friend of Frances Shand-Kydd her mother, who is rather an underestimated person. So I'm, in a way, associated with that camp.'

About Prince Charles, Runcie was less than flattering. 'It would help if he loved the Church of England a bit more... He'd go in with the *Spectator* gang on "the lovely language of the Prayer Book"', but then 'he wants to be exploring Hinduism with people in inner cities... I think he'd given up on the Church of England before I arrived.'[54]

Whereas the Charles and Diana described by Runcie are instantly recognizable as the people we know from their own self-promotions, and from the many books and articles about them, his words about the Queen are much more interesting.

Any Archbishop of Canterbury sees a lot of the monarch. And here is what Runcie said:

> The person I do admire is the Queen. She's the only person who has the ability to rise above it. I don't fully understand her, but that's part of her secret. At moments of either high drama or pressure on me – it may have been indirectly, like the papal visit or the coal miners' strike, she always went out of her way to encourage – it may have been indirectly, by an invitation to do something; it may have been by a chance word. But I've always felt that she regarded it as part of her responsibility, though he was never to be regarded as a member of the court or a private chaplain, to encourage the Archbishop of Canterbury, and to listen to what he had to say – to ask him his opinion about things. Now, I never managed to strike that sort of relationship with the Prince of Wales.[55]

Archbishop Runcie, who was a percipient man about human beings, admitted that he did not understand the Queen. She is indeed a mysterious person. It is difficult to think of anyone who has spent so much time in public life, and who remains so mysterious. In the case of Prime

Ministers, Presidents, Popes, famous actors, singers and celebrities, 'personality' of one kind or another comes through whether they want it to or not. With the Queen, very little emerges which is personal. Those who see much of her – courtiers and, sometimes, her family – speak of her warmth, or her sense of humour, or her gift for mimicry. These are not often on public display. Her great personal kindness is always mentioned. Almost the only real passion which has been revealed in public is her love of horses, and her demeanour at the races is often totally unrestrained, making the moments when photographers catch her excitement, disappointment or triumph, as a favourite horse does or does not win a race, all the more distinct.

There is one deeply personal characteristic, however, which in most human beings is private and hidden, but which in the case of the Queen has always been part of her public persona. That is her piety. And not only her piety, but the seriousness with which she regards her role as Supreme Governor of the Church of England.

In the first Christmas after her father's death, the Queen continued his tradition of making a broadcast to the Commonwealth. In those days, it was a radio broadcast, but it was done live from Sandringham, the Norfolk house where, since the reign of King Edward VII, the Royal Family have spent Christmas.

In her message, she paid tribute to her late father, and asked people to remember her at the time of her Coronation the following June.

Each Christmas, at this time, my beloved father broadcast a message to his people in all parts of the world. Today I am doing this to you, who are now my people.

As he used to do, I am speaking to you from my own home, where I am spending Christmas with my family; and let me say at once how I hope that your children are enjoying themselves as much as mine are on a day which is especially the children's festival, kept in honour of the Child born at Bethlehem nearly two thousand years ago...

But we belong, you and I, to a far larger family. We belong, all of us, to the British Commonwealth and Empire, that immense union of nations, with their homes set in all the four corners of the earth. Like our own families, it can be a great power for good – a force which I believe can be of immeasurable benefit to all humanity.

My father, and my grandfather before him, worked all their lives to unite our peoples ever more closely, and to maintain its ideals which were so near to their hearts. I shall strive to carry on their work.

Already you have given me strength to do so. For, since my accession ten months ago, your loyalty and affection have been an immense support and encouragement. I want to take this Christmas Day, my first opportunity, to thank you with all my heart.

Many grave problems and difficulties confront us all, but with a new faith in the old and splendid beliefs given us by our forefathers, and the strength to venture beyond the safeties of the past, I know we shall be worthy of our duty.

On this broad foundation let us set out to build a truer knowledge of ourselves and our fellowmen, to work for tolerance and understanding among the nations and to use the tremendous forces of science and learning for the betterment of man's lot upon this earth.

If we can do these three things with courage, with generosity and with humility, then surely we shall achieve that 'Peace on earth, Goodwill toward men' which is the eternal message of Christmas, and the desire of us all.

At my Coronation next June, I shall dedicate myself anew to your service. I shall do so in the presence of a great congregation, drawn from every part of the Commonwealth and Empire, while millions outside Westminster Abbey will hear the promises and the prayers being offered up within its walls, and see much of the ancient ceremony in which Kings and Queens before me have taken part through century upon century.

You will be keeping it as a holiday; but I want to ask you all, whatever your religion may be, to pray for me on that day – to pray that God may give me wisdom and strength to carry out the solemn promises I shall be making, and that I may faithfully serve Him and you, all the days of my life.

Six months later, on 2 June 1953, the Queen was crowned at Westminster Abbey. It was the first time that the ceremony was televised. (The choice of date had been a difficult one, since this was the first date of the Epsom meeting, and it was not known whether it would be possible to hold the Derby the next day, or whether the whole meeting should be pushed back a week – matters of urgency, not only to the Jockey Club, which decides such things, but also to the new monarch.) The Queen did not, as is sometimes stated, lead the cry for every aspect of the ceremony to be televised, but she did, when the strength of public desire for it became known, accede to the notion that the cameras should be allowed into the Abbey and that the ceremony should be broadcast live. The Archbishop of Canterbury and the Cabinet were both opposed to this, and it was the Queen who overrode them. Overnight, the number of TV licence-holders rose from 1.5 million to three million.[56]

The anointing has been part of the Coronation Ceremony since Saxon times. When the choir sang Handel's *Zadok the Priest* ('As Solomon was anointed by Zadok the priest and Nathan the prophet, so be thou anointed, blessed and consecrated Queen over the peoples whom the Lord thy God hath given thee to govern'), there can be no question that the young woman at the heart of the rite took the words extremely seriously. She is a consecrated person, an anointed monarch. In her way, a sort of priest. She regards her life as one of dedication, just as much as if she had become a nun or a member of the clergy.

Although her political views (if she has them) are opaque, her personal tastes and characteristics (outside the equestrian sphere) not so much unknown as strangely irrelevant, her conversation seldom if ever repeated, her close relationships unshared with the gossips, her religion is plainly seen as part of her role. One would guess that, as far as she is concerned, it is completely central. Certainly, at Christmas after Christmas as the years have rolled by since the Coronation, she has used the annual broadcast to testify to her faith. In 2015, reflecting on the plight of refugees fleeing to Europe from the Middle East, she said:

> It is true that the world has had to confront moments of darkness this year, but the Gospel of John contains a verse of great hope, often read at Christmas carol services: 'The light shines in the darkness, and the darkness has not overcome it'... For Joseph and Mary, the circumstances of Jesus's birth – in a stable – were far from ideal, but worse was to come as the family was forced to flee the country.
>
> It's no surprise that such a human story still captures our imagination and continues to inspire all of us who are Christians, the world over.
>
> Despite being displaced and persecuted throughout his short life, Christ's unchanging message was not one of revenge or violence but simply that we should love one another.

In the previous year, 2014, she said:

For me, the life of Jesus Christ, the Prince of Peace, whose birth we celebrate today, is an inspiration and an anchor in my life.

A role model of reconciliation and forgiveness, he stretched out his hands in love, acceptance and healing. Christ's example has taught me to seek to respect and value all people, of whatever faith or none.

Similar words could be found in any of the broadcasts she made in the 1950s. The inspiration and anchor of her life have remained constant: her faith in Jesus Christ.

This fact gives a peculiar quality to her role in regard to the Church. Many in Britain who still go to church on Christmas morning (if not very often for the rest of the year) must have come home dismayed by the lightweight attempts at humour or the patronizing secularity of the sermon by a professional member of the clergy which they have just heard from the pulpit, only to hear, in the sovereign's broadcast, the sort of words they might have expected to hear from their bishop or priest. Even if this is not the case, everyone must wonder, as the Church of England's regular congregations become more ancient and more sparse, and as Britain as a whole becomes more secular and more 'multi-faith', whether there is a place any longer for an established Church.

If you were to consult many commentators on the political scene, they would surely think that the British Head of State's relationship with the Church of England was the most anomalous feature of her role. In the course of her reign, the numbers of practising Anglicans – members of the Church of England who actually go to church – has plummeted. Runcie's successor at Canterbury, George Carey, has even suggested that the Church of which Elizabeth is the Supreme Governor, is but 'one generation away from extinction'.[57]

The National Secular Society has called for the Coronation Oath to be discarded or replaced with something 'more inclusive and appropriate for the modern era'. It reported that, in an interview, the Prince of Wales had recanted his idea that he wished to be seen as a defender of 'faiths', and he now wishes, when he takes the oath, to be seen as Defender of the Faith, as British sovereigns have been since the 1540s.[58]

When we read again the order of service for the 1953 Coronation, it is actually hard to imagine the words, as they stand on the page, ever being repeated in quite this form again. Apart from anything else, the promise to maintain the Protestant religion seems quaint, when relations between Catholics and Protestants are so much more cordial than they were when the Queen was crowned, and when the huge proportion of Christians in Britain who go to church on a regular basis are in fact Roman Catholics.

> *Archbishop.* Will you to the utmost of your power maintain the Laws of God and the true profession of the Gospel? Will you to the utmost of your power maintain in the United Kingdom the Protestant Reformed Religion established by law? Will you maintain and preserve inviolably the settlement of the Church of England, and the doctrine, worship, discipline, and government thereof, as by law established in England? And will you preserve unto the Bishops and Clergy of England, and to the Churches there committed to their charge, all such rights and privileges, as by law do or shall appertain to them or any of them?

> *Queen.* All this I promise to do.

> *Then the Queen arising out of her Chair, supported as before, the Sword of State being carried before her, shall go to the Altar, and make her solemn Oath in the sight of all the people to observe the premises: laying her right hand upon the Holy Gospel in the great Bible (which was before carried in the procession and is now brought from*

*the Altar by the Archbishop, and tendered to her as she
kneels upon the steps), and saying these words:*

The things which I have here before promised, I
will perform and keep. So help me God.

Then the Queen shall kiss the Book and sign the Oath.

*The Queen having thus taken her Oath shall return again
to her Chair, and the Bible shall be delivered to the Dean
of Westminster.*

The Church of England is often spoken about,
understandably enough, as a quasi-comic, senescent and
outmoded institution which cannot be justified, when
the majority in society do not apparently acknowledge
its place in society. Secularists, as well as religious people
who do not belong to the Church of England, might
understandably object to the hold which the national
Church still possesses on national life: the huge proportion
of primary schools (schools teaching children between
four and eleven years old), for example, are Church of
England; the most influential private schools are Church
of England foundations; nearly all the colleges at Oxford
and Cambridge have Church of England chapels and
are Church foundations too. Bishops of the Church of

England, as of right, sit (at the time of writing!) in the House of Lords. Although the statisticians seem to be satisfied that Britain is becoming ever more secular in outlook, there is no country in the Christian world, unless you count Vatican City as a 'country', where institutional Christianity is so entwined with the political framework. Can this continue?

Archbishop Fisher, who placed the crown on Elizabeth's head in 1953, recognized that the monarchy had been deprived of political power. This released it, in his estimation. It now possessed 'the possibility of a spiritual power far more exalted and far more searching in its demands: the power to lead, to inspire, to unite, by the Sovereign's personal character, personal conviction, personal example'.[59]

The Queen is an observant Anglican. She takes a personal interest in the day-to-day life of the Church of England. Archbishop Runcie's sense of support from her in times of crisis will have been felt by his successors. She has followed the changes in the liturgy and in the canon law of the Church with interest – she has always, for example, supported the ordination of women to the priesthood, and their consecration to the episcopate. More than this, however, she is that rather unusual figure on the public stage, a figure who makes her religious faith completely central to her whole world-outlook. She has been the complete fulfilment of Archbishop Fisher's dream.

Whether the future monarchs will be so overtly pious, no one can say. Whether the Church of England will even continue to exist – at any rate in its present form – is a matter of speculation. One thing can be said about the last sixty years, however, and that is that Christianity has had no more consistent public defender in British life than the Queen. She has been truly a defender of the faith, and her 'personal character… personal example' have entitled her to express her 'personal conviction'.

> God sent into the world a unique person – neither a philosopher nor a general, important though they are, but a Saviour, with the power to forgive. Forgiveness lies at the heart of the Christian faith. It can heal broken families, it can restore friendships and it can reconcile divided communities. It is in forgiveness that we feel the power of God's love…
>
> It is my prayer that on this Christmas day we might all find room in our lives for the message of the angels and for the love of God through Christ our Lord.[60]

Where else in the world do you hear such broadcasts? Even the Popes, when making their public utterances at

Christmas, usually feel they have to throw in hopes for world peace and comments on climate change or the disparity between the world's rich or poor. For the pure undiluted religious 'angle', it is in the Queen's broadcasts that one must look. As the patronage secretaries of the various Prime Ministers have considered names for future Archbishops of Canterbury, and as one unfortunate clergyman succeeded another in that unenviable role, a rather simple solution must sometimes have occurred to them. Why not double up the roles of Queen and Pontiff? Or, at the very least, why not suggest that just as Prime Ministers write the 'Queen's Speeches', the Queen should write the Archbishops' sermons?

5

BRENDA

In that red house, in the red mahogany book-case,
The stamp collection waits with mounts long dry.
JOHN BETJEMAN, 'DEATH OF KING GEORGE V'

'The press have turned us into a soap opera,'
moaned Prince Philip in 1999.[61] Some would
say, after the broadcasting of the TV film *The Royal
Family* in 1969, and as his children, throughout the 1970s
and '80s, eagerly sought to tell their version of family
squabbles to the media, that the soap opera was a joint
creation. The phrase 'royal soap opera' appears to have
been the invention of that brilliant journalist Malcolm
Muggeridge, in 1955. In a celebrated article in the
New Statesman, in September of that year, Muggeridge
wondered whether there were some people who felt
that another photograph of the Royal Family would
be 'more than they could bear'. He deplored what he

called 'the royal soap opera'. For a time it looked as if
Muggeridge, one of the best television performers in
the medium's history, would not be employable again
by the BBC. When one of his sons died at about this
juncture, Muggeridge and his wife returned home to find
the house daubed with graffiti telling him he deserved it.
At about this era, another intelligent commentator on
political and national affairs, John Grigg, was punched in
the street for daring to make some quite mild criticisms
of the Queen and the 'tweedy' courtiers with which she
was surrounded. It really seemed as if the Royal Family
were inviolable, and as if criticisms, however reasonable,
were simply not allowed.

After the truly absurd sycophancy of the 1950s,
however, things began to change. During the following
decades, very many of the distinctive features of British
life were turned on their heads. In the 1950s, for example,
those Britons who spoke with regional accents, and hoped
for advancement, were sent by their parents to elocution
lessons, where they could acquire the tones of what was
sometimes called Received Standard, sometimes BBC,
and sometimes the Queen's English (though, as we have
already observed, the Queen's particular way of speaking
English was always highly distinctive). By the 1960s, this
pattern began to change. By contrast, regional accents
and London voices were a positive advantage in many

walks of life, not just in photography, fashion or the rock music industry. Those who spoke 'posh' at home learnt to change their voices at work. Those who spoke posh all the time began to seem, if not freakish, then, a race apart. Undoubtedly, the way they spoke made the Royal Family seem strange.

Whether or not successful Roman Emperors truly employed a slave to murmur in their ears 'Memento Mori' during triumphal processions, to diminish their sense of vainglory, no such figure has been deemed necessary at the court of Queen Elizabeth II. Modern monarchs do not even require, as did their medieval or Renaissance forebears, a court fool to tease them into comparable self-realizations. Who needs a court jester when you have the press? The Fourth Estate knows that if it can pay a paparazzo to capture a royal personage sunbathing in the nude, it will sell newspapers. Royal figures are aware every day of their lives that they are 'human, all too human'. They are subjected to constant press scrutiny.

When the Queen came to the throne, the conventions surrounding the monarch, her family and their circle were rigid. When her governess, Crawfie, published the almost slavishly sycophantic *The Little Princesses* in 1950 – a behind-the-scenes glimpse of the upbringing of Lilibet and Margaret Rose – there was outcry. Crawfie was ostracized. Any member of the household who tried to 'do a Crawfie' and repeat stories of what happened when the Palace door closed would find themselves vigorously pursued by the law. Anyone who broke the code which decreed that you should not repeat conversations held with royal personages would become pariahs.

Yet, as the 1960s went by and Britain changed, it was inevitable that some embarrassment should be felt about the stuffy, old-fashioned image presented by the Royal Family, with their arcane, upper-class voices, and their apparently rarefied life of privilege. Inevitably, someone would advance the idea that they needed to 'move with the times'.

In 1969 the Duke of Edinburgh was in the United States. In an interview on NBC's *Meet the Press* he said, 'We go into the red next year, now, inevitably if nothing happens we shall either have to – I don't know, we may have to move into smaller premises... for instance we had a small yacht which we had to sell, and I shall have to give up polo fairly soon.'[62] It is not difficult to imagine the derision with which these remarks were greeted on both sides of the Atlantic. It was comparable to the moment (22 February 2006) when the Prince of Wales distributed copies of his journal (entitled 'The Great Chinese Takeaway') to some trusted friends, and it was, inevitably, leaked to the press. In this account of his journey to Hong Kong to witness the return of the colony to China, he mused, 'It took me some time to realise that this was not first class (!) although it puzzled me as to why the seat seemed so uncomfortable.' The Prince and his party had been put in the Business Class of the aeroplane because the larger First Class area was needed to accommodate the much larger party of politicians, former foreign secretaries, Prime Ministers and so forth. 'Such is the end of Empire, I sighed to myself.'[63]

No such story has ever been told about the Queen, and one suspects that it never will be. When, in late 1981, the Queen, through her Press Secretary, set up a meeting with editors and royal correspondents to discuss what she felt to be excessive pursuit of the Princess of Wales, she was asked, by the editor of the *News of the World*, 'Wouldn't it be better to send a servant to the shop for Princess Diana's wine-gums?' Her tart response was, 'Mr Askew, that was a most pompous remark.'[64]

The use of the word 'pompous' was suggestive. People might use many harsh adjectives about the Queen – stiff, unsmiling, awkward, detached – but she is not pompous. (Perhaps pomposity is nearly always a male vice?) She shares her father's quite genuine simplicity. It does not seem like 'humility', if by that is implied something affected. Ryan Parry, an undercover reporter for the *Daily Mirror*, managed to get a job for two months working as a footman at Buckingham Palace, where he snooped into bedrooms, and took photographs of private living- and dining-rooms. Among the more arresting details were the Tupperware containers which the Queen used to keep her breakfast Cornflakes. Other snaps revealed old-fashioned one-bar electric fires used to heat enormous rooms.

Her unsophisticated tastes, which were apparent to those who met her when she enlisted in the ATS during the Second World War, remained with her throughout life. Whereas most educated Britons begin their day either silently, or listening to one of two radio stations – Radio Four for its news content (the *Today* programme) or Radio Three (classical music for the news-allergic) – the Queen, together with eight million others, used to tune in to *Wake Up to Wogan* on Radio Two, a light music show cheerily hosted by the Irish broadcaster Terry Wogan. At a reception at Buckingham Palace where she showed visible delight at meeting him, she cried 'Flab!' to Wogan in reference to his 'fight the flab' campaign.[65]

There has never been any need for the Queen to pretend to a simplicity of life. True, she is on some levels a very rich woman who owns racehorses. In most respects, however, she is an embodiment of simplicity. Those who have been privy to seeing her private living quarters have seen the simplicity on display. A peer of the realm and his wife were asked to stay at Sandringham, and arrived early. They pushed open the front door and walked into the hall. The hall appeared to be empty and the peer looked around him. He had never been to the house before, and soon he began to laugh, calling out to his wife to see some fine old pictures hung on the panelling, but surrounded by appalling pastel drawings of corgis, or horses – the sort of pictures which would not even be seen for sale on the railings surrounding Hyde Park on a Sunday morning. As they allowed themselves the luxury of outright amusement, the two visitors heard a familiar voice cutting through the laughter.

'You must be Lord ******,' said the sovereign, who was sitting, quietly unseen in a corner of the hall, with an unfinished jigsaw puzzle spread out on the table in front of her.[66]

By the end of the 1960s, it was felt that she who was paraded on state occasions in a gold coach and wearing a crown should be made to reveal a more 'human' side to the public. In 1969, when the Queen was still in her early forties, a new Press Secretary, an Australian named William Heseltine, persuaded Her Majesty to allow the making of a film to be entitled *The Royal Family*. You could imagine what courtiers of the old school, such as Tommy Lascelles, would have thought of this idea, had it been suggested fifteen years earlier. It was a fly-on-the-wall documentary. The head of the documentary department at the BBC, Richard Cawston, was the director. They filmed for a year, shooting forty-three hours of footage which were edited down to an hour and a half. Here was 'the royal soap opera' indeed. Fifteen years after Muggeridge was vilified for using the phrase, now, in 1969, the Royal Family themselves seemed eagerly to embrace the role of soap opera characters.

The programme, when shown in Britain, had forty million viewers. The population of the entire British archipelago at the time was 55.44 million, so if you exclude babies and young children, the extremely old, and the numbers of people who still did not possess a television set, it would be safe to say that, in effect, almost everyone in Britain saw *The Royal Family*. It is an anodyne film when viewed today, and the details which seemed so daring in 1969 now seem merely boring. (The Royal Family attempting to light a barbecue; the Queen, Prince Philip and their two elder children at the lunch table; the Royal Family on the Royal Yacht, and so on.) In 1969, what caused the sensation was not what was shown, but the fact of it being shown at all.

Television is not a medium which easily conveys the truth. Even when it sets out to tell the truth, as Cawston's documentary did, it produces something which is by definition unnatural. It isn't natural to see a family eating a meal at which one is not a guest. And it certainly isn't natural to see a Head of State having a private conversation, however dull, about how to reply to letters from another Head of State. The unnaturalness of filming it in the first place is compounded by the voyeuristic unnaturalness of watching it. Those who had encouraged the Queen to allow the film – the modernizers such as the Duke of Edinburgh and William Heseltine – probably had the rather stupid idea that a television camera would, somehow, convey a, or the, truth – show the monarch and her family to be ordinary beings, and thereby make them more sympathetic to a possibly sceptical public. 'It wasn't a soap,' said Lord Brabourne, the film-director son of Lord Mountbatten. 'It was a matter of conveying these people as human. Before *Royal Family*, the public had no idea what they were like.'[67] Was television the best means of conveying what anyone is actually like? Was it a good idea to tell the public what the Royal Family is actually like? Has anyone ever fathomed what the Queen is actually like? ('Who are you?' asked a Malaysian boy of Prince Charles during another BBC television programme – *Charles, the Private*

Man, the Public Role, shown on 29 June 1994 – to receive the reply, 'I wish I knew.')[68]

Even at the time of the *Royal Family* film, there were sage words of caution. David Attenborough, who was famous, even in those days, for observing strange creatures in their native habitats, and using television cameras as intrusive instruments of natural history, told Richard Cawston, 'You're killing the monarchy, you know, with this film you're making. The whole institution depends on mystique and the tribal chief in his hut. If any member of the tribe ever sees inside the hut, then the whole system of the tribal chiefdom is damaged and the tribe eventually disintegrates.'[69]

We can now see that Attenborough's words were true, and that many of the more embarrassing wounds suffered by the Royal Family in the last forty years have been, if not self-inflicted, then very nearly self-inflicted. If the Queen's children, and even more children-in-law, had not chosen to co-operate with journalists in their indiscreet books and articles, they would have been in a stronger position to complain when their 'privacy' was invaded. It is hard to think of any royal broadcasts, other than the Queen's Christmas messages, and her personal message to the world after the death of Diana, which have not been disastrous. Monarchists would wish to blot from their memories, but cannot, such horrors as

It's A Royal Knock-Out (1987) organized by the Queen's youngest child, Prince Edward, in which he and his siblings, dressed in supposedly Tudor costumes, played silly games, an incident made more embarrassing by the Prince storming out of a press conference which was failing to treat him with sufficient deference. Then there was Charles's attempt to put his side of his marital troubles to Jonathan Dimbleby in the 1994 BBC programme, and Princess Diana's *Panorama* return match with Martin Bashir on 20 November 1995, in which she said she would like to be known as the Queen of Hearts... Over Princess Andrew's ex-wife's many television appearances, including her tearful appearance on the Oprah Winfrey show, kindness draws a veil. The most spectacular example of how utterly television can misrepresent reality was demonstrated in an episode of a BBC fly-on-the-wall series called *A Year with the Queen*, broadcast in 1997. One episode showed the Queen, in tiara and ceremonial robes, being snapped by the distinguished American photographer Annie Leibovitz. It would seem as if Leibovitz had also asked if she could take the Queen in something less dressy. The Queen was recorded, saying to one of her aides, 'Less dressy? What do you think this is?' Later she said, 'I'm not changing anything. I've done enough, dressing like this, thank you very much.' If this was a little bit tetchy, then anyone who has experienced the tedium of being photographed – even as the guest at a wedding – will surely recognize what tedium it must be for a public figure to undergo it on so regular a basis. The Queen was duly filmed coming into the room, dressed in these robes. In the 'edit', however, the incident changed. The Queen's completely private little complaint to her dresser became a showdown, in which she was addressing these less than civil comments to her American visitor – which she had not done. The film of the Queen, as so often looking rather cross, sweeping *into* the room dutifully for her photoshoot when she would no doubt have preferred to be elsewhere, became, in the BBC version, the Queen sweeping *out* of the room in a huff, *au* Prince Edward. The BBC, when its truly deplorable journalistic practices had been exposed, duly apologized, but it had lost the confidence of the public.[70]

The *Royal Family* film may not have been the sole cause of the change in public attitudes to royalty, but it did not help. By choosing to become, in however distant a sense, television 'personalities', the royals were placing themselves at one with any other famous person, and there was little affection or sympathy for them in the subsequent decades. The whole tenor of British life, for the last three decades of the twentieth century, was anti-hierarchical, anti-traditional, anti-deferential. It is astonishing, when one looks back on it, that it took someone (as it happens, it was Tony Blair) so long to reform the House of Lords. In November 1999, the House of Lords Act removed the automatic right of hereditary peers to sit in the Second Chamber as legislators, though some ninety-two remained, as did some bishops.

By the time this happened, the Royal Family had been through a series of calamities, culminating in the 'annus horribilis', in which, in addition to all the marital collapses, we witnessed the fire at Windsor Castle, and the sad figure of the Queen, in a headscarf and mackintosh, pacing mournfully among the smouldering ruins. Although she was a woman in her mid-sixties, she had the pathetic air of a miserable child drawn by E.H. Sheppard. It was little Lilibet among broken toys.

It was the satirical magazine *Private Eye*, inspired by the *Royal Family* film, which first called the Queen 'Brenda' and her sister 'Yvonne'. In particular Auberon Waugh, in what purported to be his diaries, constantly bemoaned the commonness of the Royal Family, claiming that the Queen sought his advice about what to do about her increasingly impossible children.

The magazine still sometimes refers to her as 'Brenda', and among a certain type of metropolitan sophisticate the nickname is still repeated. One of the remarkable things about her, though, is that almost everyone – the press, her children, her court – refers to her as 'the Queen'. When referring to the Prince of Wales, people as often as not say 'Charles'. The tabloid newspapers used to try to refer to 'Liz and Phil', but no one ever used these nicknames in real life. She is simply 'the Queen'.

If jokes have ancestry, then perhaps the 'Brenda' joke in *Private Eye* goes back to Henry James, commenting upon the death of Queen Victoria as that of the 'old middle class Queen'. In fact, Queen Victoria was not remotely middle class. In birth she was royal, European royal, through and through. In manners and custom, however, she was *sui generis*. She was truly eccentric and did not belong to any class. She was blind to class prejudice, and to race prejudice. Real members of the Victorian middle class would not, as she did, have wanted to befriend working-class men like John Brown, or brown men like her faithful Indian Muslim servant Abdul Karim. Victoria even installed Halal butchers at Windsor Castle to accommodate the tastes of Karim and his family. The Queen, our Queen, as far as we know, has no one in her life who is the equivalent of Karim, whom Victoria called 'the Moonshie'. Indeed, one of the criticisms levelled at the Royal Household years ago by John Grigg is still valid – that it is extraordinarily unmixed, racially and socially. The Queen is, however, rather like Queen Victoria, *sui generis*. Her recreations – the long weeks in the Highlands, the deerstalking, the passion for going to the races and owning racehorses – these are the recreations of the rich. Her way of doing her job, by contrast, has been to transcend class distinction. That is why the republican novelist Sue Townsend's fantasy *The Queen and I* (1992) succeeded so triumphantly on one level and failed on another. The story takes place after Britain has become a republic and the Royal Family have been made to live in a modest house on a modern housing estate in a provincial town. The novel succeeded as a plausible portrait of Elizabeth Windsor, who, together with Princess Anne, has the resourcefulness and common sense to cope with life in these changed circumstances. The book failed as the piece of republican propaganda which was originally[71] intended. Sue Townsend actually came to admire the Queen as she wrote the book. Although Townsend remained a republican, she could see that the institution of monarchy was sturdier than she had imagined, and this, in part, was something to do with the mysterious character of the Queen herself.

Reading the book, some readers will have wondered whether the deadliest legacy left to the modern monarchy by Queen Victoria was wealth. Victoria grew up, by royal standards, poor. Her widowed mother relied entirely on handouts from the King, William IV, and it was only when Victoria had become Queen that the money started to roll in. This came not, as was supposed by an increasingly hostile public, from the Civil List, but from her income from the Duchy of Lancaster. By the end of her reign, she was, in her own right, the richest person in the kingdom, even richer than the Duke of Westminster or Lord Rothschild.

Much of the unpopularity of the Royal Family stems from their wealth – Charles complaining about 'uncomfortable' seats in a section of an aircraft which most passengers could only dream about; Prince Philip considering himself poor because he might have to give up polo; Prince Andrew being given grotesque sums of money by his mother to build the hideous Sunninghill Park as a marital home with his greedy wife – whom Lord Charteris described as 'vulgar, vulgar, vulgar'. (The house has since been demolished.) And the Prince of Wales wallowing in money from the Duchy of Cornwall, and buying Highgrove as a country residence for himself, rather than moving into Sandringham, the traditional seat of the Prince of Wales since Victorian times.

Only after the 'annus horribilis' did the Queen or the Prince of Wales start to pay tax on their private income. She also agreed to strip the minor royals of their income from the Civil List and to pay for them herself – chiefly from funds from the Duchy of Lancaster.

Andrew Marr in his book *The Diamond Queen* calculates that the Queen costs the tax payer the equivalent of half a cup of cappuccino per annum.[72] This could well be true; and it is also worth bearing in mind that any Head of State, whether a monarch or an elected President, is likely to cost a lot of money – in terms of the upkeep of residences, entertaining foreign dignitaries, maintaining staff, and so forth.

There is, however, a distinction between private and public wealth. No one supposes that the state coach in which the Queen rides to Parliament is her personal property, any more than she owns the Crown Jewels in the Tower of London. Plato thought his Philosopher-Guardians, who ruled over his ideal Republic, should have no possessions at all. There would undoubtedly be a much greater purity about the relationship between the British people and the Royal Family if the Windsors were similarly dispossessed. This is not to say that they should be put into small houses on council estates, as in Sue Townsend's fantasy. Rather, that those in a direct line of succession should be dedicated beings, beings apart, from the rest of us, unfettered by actual possessions. Their houses, land, even their clothes, horses and dogs, should hold the same status as the Crown Jewels, mere accoutrements of the role. If this were to happen – a voluntary dispossession by the heir to the throne and by his heirs – much of the wind would be removed from the republican sails. The personal wealth of the Queen remains the only scandalous thing about her.

When Queen Victoria ascended her throne, the monarchs were very nearly in the position of Plato's Guardians, even if they scarcely behaved like Philosopher-Kings. They depended for money on Parliament, and they lived in their palaces as grace-and-favour dwellings, just as modern Popes, say, are placed to live in the Vatican, but do not own any of the priceless treasures in the Vatican Museums and Galleries.

That arch-royalist, and superb royal biographer, Elizabeth Longford wrote in 1993 that the only reason Prince Charles might refuse the throne would be if Parliament 'deprived him of personal independence' financially, that is, behaved as Parliaments have done ever since the reign of William and Mary. 'I think it of absolute importance that the Monarch should have a degree of financial independence from the State,' she quoted him as saying. 'I am not prepared to take on the position of sovereign of this country on any other basis.'[73]

If he still believes this, then some kind friend of his, and of the monarchy's, should urge him to think again. The colossal private wealth of the Windsors, and its abuse – witness the life and times of Charles's brother Prince Andrew, and of his estranged wife, witness the behaviour of Princess Michael of Kent, to name only a handful of examples – is the prime reason that republicanism even gets a hearing. The most sordid part of any of the books about the Windsors, past or present, is not their marital misfortunes – any decent person sympathizes with them over these, and in particular sympathizes with them having to play out their private lives on such a public stage. What sticks in the throats of many members of the public, even the most ardent royalists, is the realization that, as well as being hereditary Heads of State, the sovereigns of this House believe themselves to be somehow entitled to live like multi-millionaires. The wranglings between George VI and Edward VIII about how much rent they owed the exiled Duke for Sandringham and Balmoral (the privately owned property of the monarch), and who owned which particular jewels, snatched from Queen Alexandra's treasure-trove, make for unedifying reading.

Princess Anne is highly respected, the world over, as President of the charity Save the Children. Think what use could be made by that organization by the sale of just one item in the Queen's personal wealth – George V's stamp collection, which has probably been scarcely looked at since the 1930s.

6

PRESIDENTS

'Don't you think the PM ought to be at the north door?...
He must have more of a role, surely?'

STAFF AT NUMBER TEN, BADGERING BLACK ROD
BEFORE THE QUEEN MOTHER'S FUNERAL

Nobody quite realized, during the long premierships of Margaret Thatcher and Tony Blair, the effect that these two individuals, and their quasi-presidential style of leadership, would have on the monarchy and the British people. Under Thatcher, and even more under Blair, the British could develop a sense of what it might be like to have a President. There must be a connection between this fact and the growth in popularity of the monarchy. For, in spite of all the own goals scored by the Royal Family, in spite of their catastrophic mistakes in public relations, there can be no doubt that the monarchy, as the Queen's reign draws to its close, is more popular than ever before.

Two things might have been predicted about the

British monarchy from the late 1970s onwards. Both would have been false predictions, but they might have seemed like common sense at the time. One would have been that as Britain developed into a classless, multi-racial, pluralist European society it would have become tired of its monarchy. The public mood would decide that it was unnecessary to have a King or Queen. Why should not Britain, in common with its partners in Europe, France and Germany, have become a republic, with an elected President, serving limited times in office? Would this not be more sensible, more 'grown-up', more rational?

The other development, which would have gone hand in hand with such a public mood, would have been that the monarchy became the exclusive enthusiasm of the ultra-conservatives. In France, after the calamities of 1870, monarchism went hand in hand with politics of the extreme right. Charles Maurras, though a non-believer in God, supported the Church and believed in the restoration of the monarchy. One could imagine such a 'high Toryism' having developed in Britain – or at any rate in England, with, perhaps, T.S. Eliot (an enthusiastic reader of Maurras) as its most eloquent prophet. Eliot, it will be remembered, said, 'I am an Anglo-Catholic in religion, a classicist in literature and a royalist in politics'.[74]

Evelyn Waugh, though in a more humorous vein, tapped into a similar area of political consciousness; when asked in the 1950s how he was going to vote in a General Election, Waugh replied that he would not presume to advise his sovereign in her choice of ministers.

In fact, as the old Britain changed out of all recognition; as the class structures altered; as religion ebbed and flowed, but chiefly ebbed; and even as the Royal Family became, for long periods, objects of simple derision, the monarchy, as embodied in the person of the Queen, remained popular. The upsurge in republicanism which was sometimes predicted never took place. Those who supported monarchy no doubt included the English equivalents of Maurras, right-wing ideologues. The huge majority of those who believed in monarchy, however, as well as supporting the Queen, did not come from any narrow ideological background, but were nevertheless quite steady in their support. They came from both Left and Right of the party political spectrum.

In times when nothing stood
But worsened, or grew strange,
There was one constant good:
She did not change.[75]

Philip Larkin's quatrain for the Queen's Silver Jubilee in 1977 neatly encapsulated two contrasting phenomena. First, for conservatives such as Larkin, the great thing about the monarchy was its permanence, its unchangeability. Against this fact, there lay the uncomfortable truth that, although the monarchy did not change, the times had changed.

The Silver Jubilee itself surprised the pundits, both the republicans who believed, and the monarchists who feared, that the game was up for crowns and thrones. It was an outburst of collective merriment. It was not a celebration which specifically focused on the Queen's character, still less on the charms of her family.

In the earlier part of that year, there had seemed every reason to suppose that the Silver Jubilee would be a muted celebration, if not an actual flop. There was talk of planned street parties being cancelled for lack of enthusiasm. A political row had blown up following the passage of the 1976 Companies Act, which enabled companies to require disclosure of the true owners behind nominees' holdings in their capital. Section 27 (9) of the Act provided that a person exempted by the Secretary of State for Trade would not be obliged to comply with a notice from a company requiring disclosure.[76] An unintended consequence of the Act was that it could apply to the Queen, whose vast personal holdings could now be revealed. That is to say, the Queen's wealth – a bone of contention for many – threatened to cloud the sky. 'The exemption widens still further the gap between the Head of State and her poorest subjects,' said the director of the Child Poverty Action Group, Frank Field.[77]

The issue of poverty in Britain was a real one. So was the issue of the monarch's 'image', in particular the extravagance of her family. These would undoubtedly be matters which have remained throughout her reign, and which had to be addressed.

In 1977, however, something much simpler was demonstrated. Did the British public want, or not want, a monarchy?

It happened to be a spectacularly bright summer in 1977, after a cold, miserable spring. Soon, the street parties, which were rumoured to have been cancelled, were rescheduled. Bunting was hung from lamp-posts all over England. All over the United Kingdom, people prepared for a beano. Tony Benn attended Parliament to hear the Queen's Silver Jubilee Speech 'to remind myself of how totally undemocratic British democracy is'.[78] But what does democracy *mean* if it does not include in its definition – a system of government which people actually want?

On 6 June, the Queen climbed Snow Hill near Windsor Castle, and lit a fire as a signal for the lighting of a hundred such fires at beacons all over the kingdom. The next day, she rode in a state coach with her husband for a service of Thanksgiving at St Paul's Cathedral. More people flooded into the Mall than at the time of the Coronation. Over a million. Wherever she went during that summer, the crowds poured out into the streets. The jubilation was palpable, and the street parties were a spontaneous demonstration – not of the kind of 'monarchism' which might have appealed to right-wing theorists, such as T.S. Eliot, but of the kind of popular monarchism which was perhaps first demonstrated by Queen Victoria and Disraeli. This was not North Korea. No one was forcing us all to set up trestle tables in the streets, and to plunder our mother's cookbooks to see how to make Coronation Chicken; it simply happened, because so many of us wanted it to happen.

This was one of the very obvious facts about the monarchy which was grasped during those years by the higher echelons of the Labour movement. Harold Wilson, who had first become Prime Minister in 1964, was an instinctive politician; elected as the leftist candidate to become the Labour Leader, he was sometimes seen as a mere wheeler-dealer who knew how to keep the warring factions of the Labour Party together. A fairer judgement would be that he was an intelligent populist, with more sense of how Britain was changing, and ought to change, than his enemies credited. He struck up a warm relationship with the Queen from the first. His wife Mary (still alive aged 100 on the Isles of Scilly at the time of writing) even wrote a poem about the Queen. 'Brenda' and 'Harold' were on some levels appropriate allies. Though he was an Oxford don of modest Yorkshire origins, and her recreations included deerstalking and going to the races with aristocrats, they were both Cincinnatuses, happy with a simple manner of life, and unpompous. Both were often mocked by Auberon Waugh, in his *Private Eye* diary, the most scabrous, the cruellest and also the funniest commentary on those times. Wilson – invariably referred to as Wislon in *Private Eye* – shared with the acerbic journalist Waugh one passion which might have been the clue as to why both, in their different ways, were more in tune than many others with political mood and change: they were both keen fans of Gilbert and Sullivan. Gilbert and Sullivan made fun of British national institutions, such as the Law, Lord Chancellors, the House of Lords and, in *The Yeomen of the Guard*, the monarchy. But by no stretch of the definition were they satirists. They were essentially conservative. They saw that you can enjoy institutions and their semi-ridiculous ceremonial trappings while also revering them. 'When a great lord dies we are all diminished,' Auberon Waugh wrote in his *Private Eye* diaries. Most of his readers would have guessed this was meant as a joke, but it was not.

'I have a great respect for tradition,' Wilson told a reporter, 'I like the real ceremonies of the Monarchy… the Opening of Parliament, the Coronation. All that.'[79] There were elements in the relationship between Wilson and the Queen which were reminiscent of that between Queen Victoria and Disraeli. Dizzie harnessed the new, popular 'villa' conservatism, which had come about as a result of widening the franchise; Victoria saw that the monarchy would become more popular if she became a one-nation Tory, and an Imperialist. The symbiotic friendship between Dizzie and the Fairy enhanced both the political life of a party and of the monarchy. Similarly, the Wilson 'white hot technology' Britain did not want to discard the monarchy; it wanted the old monarchy, but one which was prepared to reform, and Elizabeth II saw this. True, Wilson was a wily man who knew that at least half his support came from the group in society which it would still make sense to call working-class Tories. There nonetheless seems every evidence that he believed this, and, moreover, that he believed in constitutional monarchy as the best possible democratic method of government. In 1966 Wilson had called a snap election, and increased the Labour majority in Parliament from four to ninety-six. The poet Christopher Logue wrote:

> I shall vote Labour because
> deep in my heart
> I am a Conservative.[80]

Wilson was succeeded by James Callaghan, the most Conservative Prime Minister since Baldwin. Callaghan confided in his friend, the Labour Party member Elizabeth Longford, 'The Queen has a deep sense of duty and responsibility in this [the political] area and also sees it as a means of preserving the Royal Family as an institution. If her Prime Minister liked to give the Queen information and gossip about certain political characters, she would listen very attentively, for she has a real understanding of the value of constitutional monarchy... I think the prestige of the monarchy would deteriorate if she did not work so hard at it... She really knows how to preserve the monarchy and how to conduct herself on public occasions.'[81]

It was Callaghan who suggested to the Queen that Prince Charles should work in Whitehall. They tried to make the Prince sit on the board of the Colonial Development Corporation, but he did not turn up to meetings. The notion that he would actually work as an intern in some Government department to see how Whitehall operated was abhorrent to the young man. 'He wasn't interested – he wanted to be a dabbler,' said one prophetic minister.[82]

The Queen's approach to her office – dutiful, inclusive, unfussy and punctilious in attention to detail – had more in common with her Labour Prime Ministers than it did with either her son's scatter-gun 'dabbler' approach to public issues or the highly divisive ideas of the monetarist 'economic liberals' who took over the Conservative Party after the fall of Edward Heath.

It was the 'conservatives' who heralded the two most radical political changes to British political life in the late twentieth century; the two changes which might most have imperilled the monarchy. The first was the Government of Edward Heath, which took Britain into the European Economic Community at the beginning of 1973. In her Christmas broadcast before this event, the Queen uttered what Ben Pimlott (the most politically astute of all her biographers) called a *cri de coeur*. 'One of the great Christian ideas is a happy and lasting marriage between man and wife, but no marriage can hope to succeed without a deliberate effort to be tolerant and understanding...We are trying to create a wider family of nations'.[83] In other words, what about the Commonwealth? The Queen evidently worried that membership of the European experiment, whose member states quite manifestly wanted 'ever closer union', would make it harder for Britain to maintain its links with the Commonwealth nations all over the world; and it would also have an immediate and deleterious effect, for example, on British trade links with the dominions. As the European butter-mountains grew, who would be buying Anchor butter from New Zealand? Pimlott tells us that the Queen, in common with the rest of the human race, found relations with Edward Heath difficult. 'Harold was fine,' a courtier recalled, 'because he loved her and treated her marvellously. But Ted was tricky – she was never comfortable with him.'[84]

What is more, the Queen's constitutional position was surely now, at the very least, questionable. If British sovereignty were to be surrendered in the interest of 'ever closer union', did this not mean that the person most affected would be the British sovereign? As things stood, in 1972, no legislature in Britain had validity until it had been signed and sealed by the Queen. All laws, passed through the two Houses of Parliament, went to the Queen for ratification. This was no longer to be the case. No one could be more aware of this than the Queen, who for twenty years had patiently worked her way through her red boxes every day, in season and out of season, overseeing the administration of the British 'thing' – whatever that was. The Queen knew more than anyone how much the sovereign was involved with the administration of Britain, even if she exercised no political sway. The removal of the uniqueness of the sovereign was not something which made much impact on public debates about European membership. Heath, however, would have been aware of it. He was an egomaniac who was intent upon stamping his image on Britain. He it was, for example, who gratuitously reordered county boundaries which had been in existence since the Middle Ages. He abolished the Assize Courts. Neither in attitude nor in deed was he 'conservative' at all, even though, when he won the leadership of his party, he had stood as the 'right wing' candidate. The further to the 'right' you are in the Conservative Party, the less conservative you are likely to be. Heath in turn was defeated by another 'right winger' – the Member of Parliament for Finchley, Margaret Thatcher, who became Conservative Leader in 1975 after Heath's humiliation at the polls. Thatcher was another non-Conservative, with absolutely no 'feel' for what made Britain British or England English. Unlike Heath, whose first job had been a reporter on the *Church Times*, she did not even belong to the Church of England. She had no experience of the country, little feeling for London, though she lived there for most of her life, no taste for Gilbert and Sullivan, almost no humour, no apparent knowledge of or pride in British industrial achievements, such as shipbuilding, glass-making, silverware, pottery, steel production – all of which declined to the point of near-extinction or actual extinction under her watch. Though she came from Lincolnshire, Tennyson's county, she never suggested a sense of place, which is something almost all British people show. In her abrasive interviews, she praised globalization and the destruction of manufacturing industries. She liked shopping malls and motorways. The old Britain, in which each town boasted its own butcher and baker and candlestick maker in the high street, was replaced by a spivs' paradise in which chain stores predominated all over the kingdom. In the election which defeated Heath, the Conservative Party had asked 'Who governs?' – meaning, should it be weird, asexual Heath, or the miners, with whom he had picked a quarrel? A grateful nation, which could remember the miners' contribution to the Industrial Revolution, and which knew that it was the miners during two world wars who had fuelled the country's power, voted out Heath. Within a decade – by 1984–5 – Thatcher had branded the miners 'the enemy within'. British soldiers, disguised by Thatcher in the uniform of the police, literally waged war on the working classes.

Admittedly, the National Union of Mineworkers now had a leader, Arthur Scargill, who was intent, as Thatcher was, upon class warfare. The Duke of Edinburgh called him 'a shit'.[85]

The Thatcher years posed a strange time for the monarchists, as for the monarch. There had been periods in history before when Prime Ministers had been more colourful characters than the King or Queen. Palmerston obviously overshadowed Queen Victoria as a 'character' who had caught the public imagination, just as Churchill was plainly a more theatrical figure than King George VI. Nevertheless, the monarch remained the monarch. When Mrs Thatcher announced that her appalling son Mark had become a father by telling the waiting reporters, 'We have become a grandmother', there must have been those who wondered what was passing through her mind.

Thatcher behaved on the political stage like a President. By now, the question of Britain's sovereignty vis-à-vis Europe had been fudged; only crazed pedants like Enoch Powell or Tony Benn bothered about it. Though in old age she became a 'Euro-sceptic', it had been Thatcher who forced through British membership of the European Union. (Just as it was the 'conservative' Thatcher, as Secretary of State for Education, who had abolished more grammar schools than the Labour Party.)

Thatcher, when finally booted out of office by her own Cabinet whose detestation of her appeared to have reached pathological levels, Britain saw its industrial base ruined, its Trade Union movement neutered, the wealth of the country dependent upon the City of London. 'Globalized' Britain meant, in essence, Americanized Britain, with Americanized values. The 1980s was a decade noted for consumerism and the polarization of society. As well as the Miners' Strike, which looked at times like a civil war, with armed police riding in charges against the strikers, whose families were quite literally going hungry, there were riots in the streets. Brixton in London and Toxteth in Liverpool erupted in flames, as discontented black youth protested, primarily because of the clumsiness of the police, but in general because of the obvious unfairness of society. In March 1990, the Poll Tax riots in London forced the Thatcher government to withdraw a proposed tax which had been forced upon the Scots, and which we can now see to be the greatest single driving force in the boosting of the Scottish Nationalist position.

Thatcher was the sort of quasi-revolutionary figure who actually needed conflict in order to succeed. Old Lady Mosley, widow of the 1930s fascist leader Sir Oswald, once said to me, 'I know one should not approve of Mrs Thatcher – because of her "monetarism" [the Fascists were keen Keynesians] – but I can't help rather liking her. She is so *just* the sort of person who joined up with us in the [British] Union [of Fascists] before the war.'[86]

You could hardly find a more direct expression of why the Queen and Mrs Thatcher were poles apart. Thatcher was not a fascist, but she had the fascist love of a fight, and the belief that confrontation and even violence were good ways of pressing home political advantage. All the Queen's instincts have been unifying ones.

The matter over which Thatcher directly clashed with the Queen was the Commonwealth. In 1979 the Commonwealth Heads of Government Conference was due to be held in Lusaka, Zambia, and the main topic for discussion was to be Rhodesia. For fourteen years it had been impossible to resolve the future of this, the most fertile country in Africa, which had made a Universal Declaration of Independence (UDI) in the time of Harold Wilson's premiership. Thatcher decreed that Robert Mugabe, President of the Zimbabwe African National Union – Patriotic Front, and Joshua Nkomo, President of the rival Zimbabwe African People's Union, were both 'terrorists'. She initially refused to attend the conference, and she did her best to make it impossible for the sovereign to attend. The Queen went and, in the words of the British Guyanan lawyer Sir Sonny Ramphal, 'brought to Lusaka a healing touch of rather special significance'.[87] The Lusaka Accord paved the way for the establishment of Zimbabwe as an independent African nation.

The Queen also clashed with Thatcher over the question of South Africa. When Her Majesty's advisers and minders want the rest of us to avert our gaze, they become a building; we are not told that the monarch's Private Secretary or her Press Secretary are embarrassed by the latest piece of tomfoolery by a royal Prince, or the newest political embarrassment. Rather, they say that 'Buckingham Palace' has taken a view upon itself. It is as if the old house, expanded to a grandiose palace, at the end of the Mall, like a little house in a children's story, has become animate, its windows winking eyes, its gateways a reproving mouth. 'Buckingham Palace' always assured us that relations between Thatcher and the Queen were of the most respectful and proper nature. Thatcher made courtiers and political colleagues giggle by the depth of her obsequious curtsies to the Queen. It was quite obvious, at the time, both that Thatcher, as power went more and more to her head, conceived of herself as the Head of State. Equally obvious was the fact that the Queen personally deplored the attitude of the Thatcher Government to South Africa.

In 1995 the Queen went to South Africa as the guest of President Mandela. It was the place where she had made her 'vow', written by Tommy Lascelles, in 1947 devoting herself to the service of 'our great Imperial family'.[88] The Queen had seen far more of that great family, which became the Commonwealth of nations, than any British politician – or, come to that, simply more than anyone else. Like Queen Victoria, who scandalized her snobbish and racist court by befriending Abdul Karim, Queen Elizabeth II was 'colour blind', though not blind to the political implications of racial tension in the world. In 1961 Harold Macmillan, the Prime Minister, had told her it was too dangerous to visit Ghana and its neo-Marxist dictator Kwame Nkrumah. Macmillan wrote in his diary, 'The Queen has been absolutely determined all through. She has great faith in the work she can do in the Commonwealth.'[89] Her visit to Ghana was a triumphant success. She scandalized Apartheid South Africa and the racist British press by dancing with Nkrumah.[90] Ghana remained part of the Commonwealth of nations. Few nowadays would commend Nkrumah, either as a man or as a politician. The Queen, however, was a bridge-builder in a way that the politicians and the journalists were not.

Likewise, in relation to South Africa nearly thirty years later. Thatcher's Government tried to stop Lancaster University giving Nelson Mandela an honorary degree while he was still in prison. Thatcher continued to defy Commonwealth opinion and to oppose sanctions to South Africa. Many in her party openly supported apartheid. Thatcher denounced Mandela as a terrorist. It was the Queen who kept faith with her friends in the Commonwealth. It was the Queen who did what seemed the decent thing at the time and, in retrospect, seems the absolutely correct thing politically: namely to see Mandela as a hero and a friend. When he returned her state visit and came to Britain in July 1996, he danced with her, and she bestowed upon him the Order of Merit, the highest honour in the sovereign's personal gift.

The Thatcher years left the British so shell-shocked that some of the electorate were credulous enough to vote in Tony Blair as a plausible alternative. Blair's attempt to use the Queen in his vulgar games of self-promotion were so transparent that they rebounded upon him. Low points included the New Year celebrations at the Millennium Dome in 1999, when he held hands with Her Majesty and tried to make her sing 'Auld Lang Syne' – her lips remained tightly closed – or when he tried to milk the death of Princess Diana by rushing to the microphones on behalf of the nation and calling her 'the People's Princess'.

Blair's desire to make political capital out of the monarchy was also on monstrous display after the death of the Queen Mother on 30 March 2002. The official known as Black Rod, who was in charge of the ceremonial at Westminster, politely told the Prime Minister's office that no particular 'role' for the Prime Minister was planned during the lying-in-state or the funeral of this much-loved royal person. Black Rod – Lieutenant-General Sir Michael Willcocks – recalled, 'Throughout the next five days, my staff and myself were telephoned, at times it seemed constantly, by staff at Number 10 repeating these questions on the role of the PM, but also exerting rather more pressure along the lines of: "Don't you think the PM ought to be at the north door?" [of Westminster Hall where the coffin lay]… "He must have more of a role surely".'[91]

Meanwhile, Blair's wife Cherie Booth QC self-importantly refused ever to curtsey to the Queen, not seeming to realize that these little rituals do not signify hero-worship of a person, but rather respect for an office and a tradition. The bad manners involved, comparable to refusal to remove one's shoes before entering a mosque, suggest a complete failure to understand why these rituals and conventions arose in the first place. Had Cherie Booth QC been lucky enough to be taken to a performance of Gilbert and Sullivan by Harold Wilson, she might have behaved less boorishly.

It would be churlish not to recognize that both Thatcher and Blair had their followers. At Thatcher's funeral, the crowds stretched all the way from St Paul's Cathedral, down Ludgate Hill and the Strand, way beyond St Clement Dane's. The BBC, which hated Thatcher, did not report this fact, but it was a palpable demonstration of her popularity. The crowds near St Clement Danes were largely Eastern Europeans who clapped her as her coffin was lifted from a motor-hearse on to a gun carriage. The crowds nearer Ludgate Circus included, I should guess, many British people who had become home-owners for the first time as a result of being able to buy their own council house or flat. Probably there were not so many attending who were now unable to obtain a council flat because so many had been sold off during the Thatcher years.

We do not know yet how many will attend Tony Blair's funeral. The British experience of having the Thatcher years followed by the Blair years actually had a profound effect on the British people's relationship with the monarchy.

In the Queen's Golden Jubilee year – 2002 – in which she lost both her mother and her sister, she visited seventy British towns and cities. 'Gratitude, respect and pride, these words sum up how I feel about the people of this Country and the Commonwealth – and what this

Golden Jubilee means to me.'[92] That was what she said in the Guildhall, having been conveyed there in a gold state coach. The people reciprocated, with apparently over 200 million watching the Jubilee celebrations on television worldwide. In Britain the gratitude was positive – gratitude to a woman who had been so faithful to her calling for fifty years. It was also, in part, negative. A high proportion were grateful that she was neither President Thatcher nor President Blair.

7

DOES THE MONARCHY
HAVE A FUTURE?

Chris Mullin MP, showing Prince Philip the
ultra-modernist design of the new GCHQ building in
Cheltenham: Would Charles approve?

Prince Philip: Charles who? [93]

Larkin's lines on the Queen's Jubilee were perhaps less famous than his poem 'Annus Mirabilis', which dated the change in sexual *mores* to 1963:

Between the end of the Chatterley ban
And the Beatles' first LP.

Larkin was a passionate monarchist, but he also envied the emotional and erotic freedoms of the young. For the monarchist, there is a paradox here. In the merry old days of yore, when we of the middle and lower classes were expected to disguise our sexual feelings behind a carapace of conventions, it was, supposedly, the upper classes, and royal personages, who could get away with behaving as libertines. Even a cursory reading about the life of Louis XIV's court at Versailles, as described in the pages of the Duc de Saint-Simon, would make you think that Britain in the Swinging Sixties was comparatively strait-laced. Likewise, if you read Roger Fulford's *Royal Dukes* (1933) about the sons of George III, you would think that no modern royal scandal could match the way in which the self-indulgent and, on the whole, rather nasty uncles of Queen Victoria chose to behave.

Today, the boot is on the other foot. We've all changed, and it is the Royal Family who are supposed to keep the suburban virtues of the 1950s vintage. Newspapers express mock amazement if they do not. A Prince in a nightclub, half tight and dancing with a good-time girl? Perfectly normal for Edward VII or Edward VIII but apparently shocking for Prince Harry. The phrase 'living in sin', to describe a man and a woman who shared a house without being married, was commonplace in the 1950s. Now, almost all young people consider it not merely natural, but proper not to marry the first person to whom they feel attracted. Sin does not come into it. When the Queen came to the throne, consenting gay men would be sent to prison, and the law only changed gradually, during the Labour Governments of Harold Wilson, under the benign Home Secretaryship of Roy

Jenkins. It is all so recent, and yet, for anyone under the age of forty, it must seem all but unimaginable. Now, it is the fortunate who find that they are still happily married to the same partner throughout their lives; and when a marriage breaks down, or fizzles out, or whatever the appropriate metaphor might be, the ethos of the age would suggest that it was more seemly to bring such an unhappy union to an end in as 'civilized' a manner as possible, than to struggle on in what John Milton, that seventeenth-century advocate of divorce, called 'a drooping and disconsolate household captivity'.

The sexual revolution placed the Royal Family in a very difficult position, not least because it coincided with a growth in the power of the British press, the collapse of the culture of deference, and the disappearance, really, of any conventions by which figures in public life might be protected from intrusion by the cameras or pens of journalists. Whereas the Queen's generation, and that of her parents, were bound by strict marital conventions, they were also protected by strict press conventions. 'Everybody knew' about the behaviour of, let us say, the Queen's uncles, the Duke of Kent, or Lord Mountbatten, whose marriages were far from being models of middle-class rectitude. Equally, though Everybody knew, Nobody would have printed the stories in the newspapers; it would have been quite unthinkable. Throughout 1936, when *le tout Londres* spoke of Edward and Mrs Simpson, the newspapers said nothing. Those with an eye for social change would have seen that *Private Eye*, in the early 1960s, changed the atmosphere forever. Its repeated hints, for example, about Lord Mountbatten's bisexuality were regarded as the worst of bad taste. They also changed the way the public expected to read royal news. While the conventional press continued to lard the Royal Family with flattery, the *Eye* – and the TV satirists of *That Was The Week That Was* – made them objects of derision; and, as such, fair game – that cruel, monosyllabic phrase which usually denotes its opposite. Merely being born royal now made the press feel entitled to spy upon them, and report all the matters which, in a normal human life, are kept hidden.

The Queen's children were to grow up into an unfair world, where all their emotional mistakes were regarded as fair game by the Fourth Estate. The great public came to terms with the revolution in sexual ethics, except in relation to the Royal Family. The public – most of them, it would seem, anyway – wanted a relaxation of the old morality. They wanted to be free to fall in and out of love, to have more than one partner in the course of their lives, and to demand the freedom before the law to behave as they liked, provided that 'they' were mutually consenting adults. Here, the public – or at any rate, the scandalous newspapers which they eagerly purchased in huge numbers – wanted things both ways. Their own private lives could remain as private as they chose, and could be as emotionally chaotic as they chose. Perhaps partly for this reason, they wanted the royal marriages to be 'fairy tales', just as some roués tearfully devote themselves to the Blessed Virgin. When the reality of royal 'fairy tales' became apparent, the press responded with a prurient severity which they would not have visited upon pop singers or film stars.

'We had the good fortune to grow up in happy united families,' the Queen said in a speech at the Guildhall to mark her silver wedding in 1972. 'We have been fortunate in our children, and above all we are fortunate in being able to serve this great country and Commonwealth.'[94] As far as her husband was concerned, this was a piece of pious fiction – he had not grown up in a happy family. Indeed, if you wrote down a short biography of Prince Philip on a piece of paper without mentioning that he was royal – 'born on a kitchen table of impoverished refugee parents; mother certifiably insane; father deserted the marital home; child the youngest of a rum brood, one of whose sisters married a keen and practising Nazi; brought up in a Scottish boarding school by punishment freaks, and only occasionally seen by unsympathetic grandparents' – you would think that he should, rather than being sent to Gordonstoun, have been taken into care. Perhaps, in a sense, that was what his marriage was? Perhaps for all his strutting claims as a young man that he found the burden of being second fiddle to his wife hard to bear, and the abandonment of his naval career a sad deprivation, he actually needed the disciplined and restricted life which being the Duke of Edinburgh imposed upon him?

Lilibet's childhood had, by contrast with her husband's, evidently been happy, and her father's letter to her upon her marriage to Prince Philip would be regarded as touching even by the most steely hearted: 'Our family, us four, the "Royal Family" must remain together.'[95]

The stability of 'us four' enabled the Royal Family to put behind them the nightmare of the Abdication. Was there a little hubris in the Queen's repetition of 'we are fortunate', in that speech of 1972? The innocent domestic simplicity which was exemplified and enjoyed by her father and mother could not realistically be reproduced in the marriages of her sister or of her children. In 1976 Princess Margaret and her husband Lord Snowdon were separated after sixteen years of marriage. On 24 May 1978 the Princess was granted a decree nisi by the Law Courts in London, and became the first member of the British Royal Family to obtain a divorce since George I dissolved his marriage to Princess Sophia of Celle. (The newspapers wrongly said it was the first royal divorce since the reign of Henry VIII; they also overlooked George IV's very public, if unsuccessful, attempt to divorce Caroline of Brunswick.) Until the end of Princess Margaret's marriage, it had been possible to maintain the old conventions: those who married the divorced, as Edward VIII so fatefully had done, could not expect to be presented at the twentieth-century court, or even to be admitted to the Royal Enclosure at Ascot. Now came the woeful roll-call of the Queen's children and their marital misfortunes: Princess Anne, married 1973, divorced 1992; Prince Andrew, married 1986, divorced 1996; Prince Charles, married 1981, and also divorced 1996. (His wife Diana was killed in the Paris motor smash the following year.) Statistically, the Royal Family scores highly – anyway by British standards – in its divorce rate; it is easily on a level with Beverley Hills, perhaps in part for similar reasons – only a certain type of person would wish to marry either a famous film star or a member of a royal family, and one of the qualifications would, normally, be stupidity. For who would choose – actually choose – to abandon privacy?

Each of those failed marriages – Margaret, Anne, Andrew and Charles – were played out in circumstances which any normal, private person would have found intolerable. It is truly remarkable, the embarrassing personal details about all of them which were fed into the public consciousness. Any one of these stories, if told about ourselves or our children to a wider public, would be enough to induce nervous collapse in a normal family. For the Queen's sister and her children – who were not necessarily the cleverest or strongest people in the world – it became part of the everyday fabric of experience that the public should know not merely the bare fact that their marriages had failed, but quite prodigious amounts of detail, about their verbal quarrels, their love affairs, their foibles.

Very occasionally, as when Princess Margaret appeared in her last illness, being pushed in a wheelchair with a swollen face and dark glasses, or, most extreme of all, when Diana was killed in Paris, the blood-lust of the press would be shamed into a shocked silence... For a day or two. On the whole, however, the lust remained insatiable, with long-ranged photographic lenses and phone hacking making it possible for the press to intrude to an extent which would have been impossible in an earlier age – even if 'deference' had not made such intrusions unthinkable. With the coming of the Internet, the days of print journalism appeared to be threatened, if not altogether numbered, and like a wild beast snarling with ever greater ferocity in its dying gasps, it seemed not to care how cruelly it behaved. Phone hacking was only the part of it.

The existence of such journalistic tricks, combined with a perceived 'right to know' the financial secrets of famous figures, has had a devastating effect on the political and public life of the Western world. In the past, a clever or gifted person could aspire to a position in public life without feeling that they, and their children, would lose all privacy. He or she who chooses to become a politician in today's Western world, with 'freedom of information' and a journalistic 'open season' on what was once 'private life', is either unusually blameless or so ambitious as to be brazen. Clearly, it has led to the withdrawal of very many men and women of talent from the public stage, who would prefer to work as financiers, lawyers, writers and business-people than to put themselves and their families through the hell of perpetual exposure.

The hereditary monarch and her family do not have this luxury. When they behave oddly, which they quite often seem to do, it is worth remembering that they are now living lives which most of us would be unable to endure. The Queen has been largely protected from the full glare of journalistic publicity, the only aspect of her private affairs to which attention is drawn from time to time, being the all but impenetrable area of her personal finances. Because the Queen is spared, the Duke of

Edinburgh is spared. Although they may think that they suffer an intrusive press, what they have suffered has been nothing compared with the scrutiny which has been directed, in season and out of season, at their four children and their spouses, and their grandchildren.

This fact is so overwhelming that it overshadows any consideration of whether the Queen and Prince Philip have prepared the next generation to be monarchs for the future.

Most people are agreed that the Queen has performed her tasks well throughout her reign, and – with the inevitable provisos about the 'gaffes' – everyone agrees that Prince Philip has been a loyal and dutiful consort, though never the Prince Consort in name. The Queen's task, however, is not merely to be a constitutional monarch, but to prepare that institution for the future.

If monarchs had a statutory retirement age at, say, seventy, which no law could alter, they would perhaps have a different relationship with their heirs. As it is, any reigning monarch, looking at the heir apparent, will think, 'You are waiting for me to die. Until I do so, you have no function, other than functions which you have dreamed up for yourself.'

The Hanoverians have been spectacularly bad about this. Think back only as far as George III, who made no secret of detesting the future George IV. Queen Victoria's dislike of Bertie, the future Edward VII, was no secret. Indeed, it was only by the Queen attending a public service of thanksgiving at St Paul's for his recovery that the monarchy began to be popular again. George V hated and bullied Edward VIII, and perhaps if he had not done so, Edward would not have felt a compulsion to pull down the whole house of cards by abdicating.

By the standards of their forebears, the Queen and Prince Charles have not made too bad a fist of this difficult relationship, monarch and heir. Prince Charles from time to time made public, or semi-public, declarations that his parents had not loved him enough as a child, using Jonathan Dimbleby's *The Prince of Wales: A Biography* as a vehicle to suggest that the Queen had been cold and Prince Philip a bully. That was in 1995, and many years have passed since then. The Prince of Wales has made many gallant allusions to his mother and his speech to her at the Diamond Jubilee in which he called her 'Mummy' (perhaps one should spell that 'Mummie') was surely rather touching, the more so if he does not actually call her 'Mummie' in private. (The Duke of Edinburgh's leaked letters to Diana suggest that the Prince and Diana were encouraged to call her 'Ma'.)

It is a fair question, whether the Queen has been a 'good mother'. Much more to the point is whether she and her husband have enabled her heir, and his heirs, to carry on as plausible constitutional monarchs in the future. One comes back to Queen Mary's dismay at the poor education of her own husband, George V.

If they were to look back, Prince Charles's parents might think that they made a mistake in selecting the hellish Scottish boarding school Gordonstoun. He was evidently very unhappy there, and it could scarcely have been a good preparation for acquainting himself with the life of the kingdoms he was to govern. Since then, however, Charles went to Cambridge, and he has also had a wide and varied experience, both of friendship at every level of society, and of social usefulness. The Prince's Trust has helped thousands of young people into work. His sponsorship of an art school – The Prince's Drawing School in Shoreditch (now the Royal Drawing School with three other London sites) – was also an imaginative and bold thing to do at a moment in British history when many of the mainstream art schools had all but given up on teaching the traditional skills of draughtsmanship. Pricked by the example and success of the Prince's school, many art schools have gone back to teaching their students to draw.

Whether or not you agree with the Prince of Wales's many views on architecture, on the environment, on the place of the faiths in public life, and on so much else, it could hardly be argued that he has not been deeply engaged with his mother's realm, in a way which has neither bitten impatiently at her heels, nor implied criticism of her very different way of being a royal personage. Those who dislike Prince Charles's way of engaging with public life – writing 'black spider memos' (so called because of the supposed resemblance of his handwriting to spidery-spinnings) to Government ministers about matters of the day, for example, or using his very considerable influence to promote highly contentious architectural views – like to say that the Queen has been very 'worried' by his outspokenness; consider it likely that he would imperil the future of the monarchy; wish he would imitate her habits of restraint and silence. One day, perhaps, her diaries will be published and we shall know what she actually thought about her son and heir. Given her way of conducting herself, however, it would not be surprising if her diaries turn out to be as restrained and impenetrable as she has been in person.

While it is not necessary to pass judgement on the Queen's maternal skills, as, by implication, *The Prince of Wales: A Biography* did, it is surely legitimate to look at the Queen's children and ask – Does the monarchy have a plausible future? The general consensus seems to be that Princess Anne is a sensible, down-to-earth, unpompous person, who has done good things with Save the Children, and would have made an excellent monarch had her brothers not existed. This view can sometimes be voiced as a positive expression of admiration for the Princess Royal, and sometimes as a none too subtle judgement on her brothers. The characters of Prince Andrew and Prince Edward might be of interest to those who follow the 'soap opera', but they are not directly relevant to those who ask whether the British monarchy has a future. All that matters, in that regard, is whether the institution can plausibly be carried on by the Prince of Wales and his descendants.

Let us give a very simple disyllabic answer to that question – Why Not?

The monarchy could be imperilled if the occupant of the throne, or the next in line, started to behave in such a grossly inappropriate way that public opinion simply would not stand for him, or her, as Head of State. Let us suppose in the rather unlikely event that the Prince of Wales's leaked letters to politicians were full of racist abuse, or that he turned out to be an enthusiastic and unashamed paedophile. Needless to say, we are a very long way from this.

It is a mistake to confuse the popularity of the Prince, or of his son or grandson, at any one moment in the newspapers, and the popularity of the idea of monarchy.

Clearly, the two are connected, for if the Royal Family were not merely treated with healthy British disrespect and derision much of the time, but instead with outright hatred and contempt, then they would be in trouble. That is because, in the end, the monarchy only survives in Britain for one reason. People want it to do so.

One of the reasons that the Queen's custodianship of a constitutional monarchy has been so successful is that she has not been the object of any kind of personality cult. Indeed, her personality, as such, remains totally mysterious, not only to the public, but to many who think they know her best. Her, on occasion, flashes of good humour, her dutifulness, her virtue, her unchangeability – these are not, as such, 'qualities'. There was a long, ironical Austrian novel called *The Man Without Qualities*, and it could be said that Elizabeth II was 'the Queen Without Qualities' – if by 'quality' is meant a characteristic which you would say was 'typical' of them. Even though so few of us have met any of the Royal Family, we all know – and are certain of the rough accuracy of our knowledge – what Prince Charles and Prince Philip and Princess Anne are 'like'. You could not make any such statements about the Queen beyond listing the same curious pastimes – dog-walking, jigsaw puzzles and going to the races, combined with religion and a passionate devotion to duty.

This makes the impersonal machine of Government work much more easily than it could do with a more pronounced 'character'. Probably, had George VI's tantrums or George V's outbursts of rage and sailor's language been known to the public, it would have changed public perceptions; but, of course in those days the newspapers would never have reported them.

What personal characteristics of any future monarch – Charles, William or George – will or won't be helpful to the future preservation of the institution, this we must leave to the future to decide. What we can do, in the remaining two chapters of this book, is to answer the question – Why Not? Why should Britain *not* continue to be what it has been since the time of the Saxon Kings, a monarchy, since the Norman Kings, an hereditary monarchy, and since Victorian times, a constitutional monarchy?

Why should the Prince of Wales and his descendants *not* hand on the monarchy to the future, as George VI handed it to Elizabeth and Elizabeth to her heir?

Strangely enough, in the twentieth and twenty-first centuries, British republicans have been fewer proportionately than they were in the nineteenth century, when Queen Victoria's supposed idleness and withdrawal from public duty encouraged the revival of older republican views. In 1899 many Members of Parliament had tired of all the monarchist enthusiasms of the two Jubilees and it was with joy that they commissioned the sculptor Hamo Thornycroft to make a giant image of Oliver Cromwell – one of his best – which they defiantly erected outside the Houses of Parliament. This also had the added bonus, for some of the more belligerent parliamentarians, of infuriating the Irish.

The Victorians in large numbers felt the attraction of the republican idea. The idea has never died in Britain and it would not take much to make it flicker back into popularity. Suppose the Royal Family themselves, worn out by over-exposure in sadistic newspapers, reached a point where enough was enough, and they chose to step down; and the mood in the country at large – perhaps by then, a country divided, with a separate Ireland, Scotland and Wales – was republican? Britain was a republic once before – from 1649 to 1660. Could it, should it, not be a republic again?

8

THE GOOD OLD CAUSE

'I did desire to speak for the liberties of England.'
CHARLES I AT HIS TRIAL

'[Colonel Harrison] went to his death with equanimity, the first
of the Regicides to suffer. The crowd was hostile and derisive.
"Where is your Good Old Cause now?" they jeered. "Here in my
bosom," said Harrison, "and I shall seal it with my blood".'
C.V. WEDGWOOD, THE TRIAL OF CHARLES I[96]

In some countries, the civil wars of the past repeatedly resurface. In France, the defeat of the monarchy and the decapitation of large numbers of its aristocratic adherents in the period between 1789 and 1793 is a gruesome melodrama which is re-enacted over and over again. You see it in the convulsions of 1830 and 1848. You see it at the time of the catastrophe of the German war in 1870. You see the divisions reappearing during the Dreyfus affair, and you see it in the reactions to 1940.

Those who supported the King and/or the Church in 1789 were resurrected to fight the old battles – or, in the case of 1940, not to fight.

Similar echoes can be seen from time to time in the United States when the old South finds itself forcibly reminded of its defeat at the hands of the Federal Government in 1865 – witness the relatively recent outlawing (by the Senate of South Carolina in July 2015) of the Confederate flag, following the murder of nine black people at a church in Charleston.

The English Civil Wars left a paradoxical legacy (I use the word 'English' advisedly – perhaps the recent election of fifty-seven Scottish Nationalists out of fifty-eight possible Scottish Parliamentary seats in Westminster tells its own story). One benign way of looking at them is to think that, when the monarchy was restored in 1660, that merry monarch Charles II healed all the wounds of the previous eleven years, and, by his judicious toleration of the Puritans, he taught the English to forget their differences. Another view is that those who had supported the Parliamentary cause (at any rate in the early stages of the First English Civil War), those who would become the Whigs, sort of won. Charles II came back on sufferance of the Army, and he could not have governed without what became the Whig establishment. When his brother James II 'went too far'

– by trying to force the universities to accept Roman Catholic appointees, and by evidently undermining the very concept of the Church of England – he was in effect dismissed. Certainly, no monarch since crowned in Westminster would have been able to suppose for a moment that they were absolute rulers in the old Stuart or Bourbon pattern. 'The Good Old Cause' saw to that. How far, however, has the Good Old Cause got to run? In our own day, is the republicanism which slept in 1660 due for arousal?

On 25 January 2016 General David Morrison, the former Head of the Armed Forces in Australia, threw his support behind the Australian Republican Movement, whose aims and intentions are clearly spelt out for anyone who joins the cause: 'We as Australians affirm our allegiance to Australia and its people, whose democratic beliefs we share and whose rights and liberties we respect. We propose, as a great national project involving all our citizens, that Australia becomes an independent republic with one amongst us chosen as our Head of State.'[97]

There can be no doubt that the Australian Republican Movement is gaining ground in that country, and that more and more Australians, many of whom are not of

British descent, see no reason why the British monarch should be their unelected Head of State.

The Queen recognizes this. Back in 1999, when Paul Keating, Australia's Labour Prime Minister, put the matter to the vote, the result was 55 per cent in favour of the status quo and 45 per cent in favour of a republic. But that was nearly twenty years ago. When a figure like General Morrison – who has, after all, sworn an oath of allegiance to the Queen as his Head of State – comes out as an uncompromising republican, something has definitely happened: he said he was 'proud' to lend his voice to the cause.

'With great respect to those who don't share my views and recognizing our proud history of European settlement in this country and beyond, over 200 years and more, I will lend my voice to the Republican movement in this country,' he said. 'It is time, I think, to at least revisit the question so that we can stand both free and fully independent amongst the community of nations.'[98]

'I committed my life to the service of the Commonwealth,'[99] the Queen said in Durban at the fiftieth anniversary Commonwealth Heads of Government meeting. Yet, as everyone present on that occasion knew,

Elizabeth's commitment had been made in very different circumstances. Nor was her commitment, when she spoke the words, to a 'Commonwealth': it was to an Empire. It was in Cape Town in 1947, on a visit to South Africa with her parents, the King and Queen, and her sister Princess Margaret. The visit coincided with her twenty-first birthday, and she made a broadcast, not to the Commonwealth, which did not yet exist, but to the Empire.

> There is a motto which has been borne by many of my ancestors – a noble motto, 'I serve'. Those words were an inspiration to many bygone heirs to the throne when they made their knightly dedication as they came to manhood. I cannot do quite as they did.

> But through the inventions of science I can do what was not possible for any of them. I can make my solemn act of dedication with a whole Empire listening. I should like to make that dedication now. It is very simple.

> I declare before you all that my whole life, whether it be long or short, shall be devoted to your service and the service of our great Imperial family...

No one could doubt either the sincerity of the young woman who made this vow, nor, even more impressively, the fact that the ninety-year-old woman who is still committed to her role as Head of the Commonwealth has been tireless in fulfilling the role. She has been what two commentators astutely named 'the benign Great Mother'.[100]

In South Africa, where the speech was made, it was always felt that there was a bond between 'the Head of the Commonwealth and liberal opinion'.[101] President Mandela, on his state visit to Britain in 1995, made it clear how warmly he felt towards the Queen for her support for the Commonwealth – in the face of Margaret Thatcher and the Conservative Party's suspicion of Mandela and opposition to sanctions in the apartheid years. Indeed, one of his first acts as President had been to apply for the democratic Republic of South Africa to be readmitted to the Commonwealth, after its long years in the wilderness.

The Commonwealth is a strange anomaly. It could not exist had not the Empire once existed. Many of its members, however, including the independent republics such as South Africa, value the co-operation of its members and feel that they can achieve things together which would not be possible apart.

The United States of America declared itself to be an independent republic in 1776. The Irish Free State, which was a dominion of the British Commonwealth from 1922 to 1937, ratified a new Constitution in 1937 and became an independent republic.

There comes a point when children are children no more, and when they do not wish to have a 'Great Mother', however 'benign'. In Canada, Jamaica, New Zealand, as in Australia, there are vigorous movements to follow the way of Ghana in 1960, Nigeria in 1963, or Zimbabwe – which eventually became a republic, under the presidency of the Reverend Canaan Banana in 1980, after fifteen years of uncertain international status following the UDI of the government of Ian Smith ('Smithy').

The Empire became a Commonwealth of loosely federated independent states and some dependencies. If, as would seem to be overwhelmingly probable, the remaining countries of the Commonwealth declare themselves to be republics in the future, we could ask what future there could, or should, be for a monarchy in the 'Mother Country'.

One of the most eloquent, and certainly one of the best loved, exponents of British republicanism in recent years was Tony Benn – the Right Honourable Anthony Wedgwood-Benn, Viscount Stansgate, call him what you will. He inherited a viscountcy from his father who had been a Labour MP like himself and who was ennobled by Clement Attlee, and lurched, as a 'moderate' member of the Labour Party, to being the firebrand of the supposedly 'extreme' leftists in the movement. Fascinatingly, Benn set out to become not merely the darling of the Left, but the darling of almost everyone else in Britain as well. Audiences on such radio shows as *Any Questions* are composed of a wide range of political opinions, and would receive firmly left-wing views from other political speakers with a mixture of emotions. When Benn spoke, however, calling for the abolition of the House of Lords, or of the monarchy, and the introduction of, in effect, Communist controls of the economy, the audiences would erupt into the sort of rapture normally reserved for pop idols. However often he repeated his anecdotes, they laughed and cheered, as if they had never heard the ancient jokes and watchwords before – or perhaps because they had heard them, and enjoyed the almost liturgical reassurance of repetition, like the after-dinner stories of a favourite uncle. Of course, republicanism was a *sine qua non* of his creed. He never played this down to those audiences, and when he attacked the hereditary principle, or the inequalities encouraged in Britain by having a monarch, he always received thunderous applause.

Benn was a gentle figure, and was never personally ill-mannered or unkind about anyone, least of all about his monarch. His version of republicanism was not personally vindictive, and it is one which surely needs to be addressed, since it cut to the nub of why the British monarchical system is so profoundly offensive to significant numbers of British citizens.

In one of the endlessly repeated rehearsals of his views of life, Benn would recall the example of his mother, a keen Bible-reader who liked to tell him that the Bible was the story of Kings and Prophets. The prophets were called by God to hold the Kings to account – and this was clearly – though he had abandoned a formal allegiance to Christianity – how Benn saw his role, and that of the Left in Britain: holding Kings to account.

Clearly, what was meant by this was holding the Powerful to account. What Benn fundamentally objected to was not the concept of Kings and Queens, but the notion of power being held in the hands of the unelected. 'The fount of honour has been re-routed from Buckingham Palace and now sprays the holy water of patronage on the chosen few from 10 Downing Street, which appoints archbishops, bishops, cabinet ministers, peers and judges and fills most senior government posts with the people it wants,' Benn wrote in *The Guardian* on 11 November 2003. 'Declarations of war and Britain's adherence to treaties such as the new European constitution are exercised under prerogative powers by the prime minister who may or may not choose to consult the Commons or the electorate in a referendum.'

This is a trenchantly expressed critique of the way in which Government exercises power in the United Kingdom. It raises two questions, however, in the minds of those who attend to it.

Is it actually a criticism of monarchy, or merely of unaccountable Government?

Secondly, would Government be more accountable if the monarchy were abolished?

Benn's criticism of unaccountable Government is broadly speaking true. Quentin Hogg (Viscount Hailsham), Lord Chancellor in Margaret Thatcher's Government, belonged to the opposite side of politics, but it was he who described the British system of Government as an 'elective dictatorship'. Once a party has won an election in a British General Election, and commands a majority in the House of Commons, its 'elective' function is forgotten for five years. The Prime Minister, any Prime Minister, leading such an administration does indeed exercise the power which politeness attributes to the Crown. Everything from the endorsement of international treaties to appointments to minor committees in what is loosely speaking 'public life' is influenced, or directly controlled, by Downing Street.

Yet, as Benn made clear, 'They cling to the monarchy, and would be ready, as in 1936, to ditch the King himself.'

Those who believe themselves to be monarchists do not always grasp this point, and Benn made it very clearly. Benn was right to see 1936, and the Abdication, as a revelatory moment in British public life. In case no one had got the message in 1689, when the monarch was sacked by the Whig aristocracy, Britain has had Heads of State who are, in effect, puppets through which others exercise the real power. In the period 1689 to 1832, those who exercised power were, quite literally, a handful of powerful landed families. In later times, it has been that amorphous but very real body known as the Establishment which exercises power. It is, moreover, perfectly true that monarchs who do not dance to the Establishment's tune are very easily disposable: witness the dismissal of Edward VIII. Listen to the way 'they' at London dinner parties – men in clubs, politicians of Left or Right in the corridors of Westminster – speak about the Prince of Wales if his 'interference' in public affairs strikes 'them' as indiscreet.

That 'the Establishment' runs Britain is not in doubt, and the fact that you could not exactly specify who were members of it, and what it is, does not invalidate such a statement. And that the existence of 'the Crown' perpetuates and helps such a system is also every bit as true as Tony Benn believed.

He is no longer here to answer for himself, but those who are convinced by his particular brand of republicanism need to answer a few points and questions.

First, corruption. The Corruption Perceptions Index, an international body which monitors such questions as bribery in public office, does not consider Britain to be an especially corrupt nation. In its index of world nations in 2015, Britain came twelfth, and of the nations which were even less corrupt in public life, incidentally, eight were constitutional monarchies – Denmark, Sweden, New Zealand, the Netherlands, Norway, Canada and Luxembourg. One could make objections to the monarchical system, therefore, but it seems unreasonable to suggest that having such a system is inherently unfair, or likely to produce privilege gained in some back-handed or corrupt manner. One reason for this in Britain is that the Civil Service is 'above politics', and, as invented and reformed by the Victorians, is detached from party politics. The lack of corruption does not, therefore, descend from the Crown, but nor could it be shown that the Crown encourages favouritism or corruption of any kind, when it comes to making important public appointments.

Further – Benn's idea that the Crown appoints many such public figures is true, but it would be fanciful in the extreme to suppose that 'the holy water of patronage' was 'sprayed' as in the old days when, for example, officers bought their commissions in the British Army, or courtiers and politicians did accept bribes to offer promotion. In the armed services, appointments are clearly made with at least the intention of choosing the best person for the job. It would be ludicrous to suggest, as Benn did, that the judiciary was 'sprayed' with 'holy water', and that judges were appointed from the ranks of Government apparatchiks; quite the contrary, the judiciary in Britain has a good tradition of holding the Government to account, and, for example in the area of human rights law, frequently infuriating both politicians and the Conservative press by decisions from the bench. Long may this continue.

Opinions might differ about whether or not the Crown should appoint bishops and deans, but, again, only in Benn's dream-land are these appointments made with any political or sinister intention. The reality of the matter is that the Church keeps its own eye on who it wants to be its senior administrators, and there are very few British politicians who would have the competence or the desire to 'place' favourites into deaneries and bishoprics, as they might have done in the days of Anthony Trollope.

The Establishment does exist, yes. But the institutions which form part of this nebulous body of men and women – the universities, the judiciary, the Church, the Civil Service, the BBC and the higher ranks of 'serious' journalism – are not in any realistic sense affected by the Crown, still less in an actual sense by Queen Elizabeth II herself.

Furthermore, Bennite republicans would have difficulty in persuading me that a republican style of government in Britain would necessarily be freer or more open. True, in an ideal, beautiful world, it might be possible for every member of a quango, every Governor of the Bank of England or of the BBC, every Principal in the Civil Service, every university Vice-Chancellor only to be there by popular acclamation or election, but it is to be doubted whether many people would turn out to vote for such figures; and even more doubtful whether the characters occupying these (usually very boring) positions would in fact have an identity which differed from those who occupy them at present. It is true that the House of Lords is a shambles, but the way in which Tony Blair as Prime Minister (and, to a numerically smaller degree, David Cameron) cheerfully packed the second Chamber with their own stooges does not reflect poorly on the monarchy – we all know that this sort of shabby political influence would be more powerful, not less, without at least the theoretical restraints imposed by the Crown.

A footnote to Andrew Marr's *The Diamond Queen*. He quotes the (unintentionally) comic episode in Tony Benn's Diaries (10 March 1965) in which Benn, at the time the Government Minister responsible for the design of new postage stamps, had an audience with the monarch. Until this point in history all stamps and coins bore the head of the sovereign and Benn, as what Marr calls a 'soft' republican 'at this stage',[102] went to the Queen with designs for some stamps to commemorate the Battle of Britain. The designer was another republican, David Gentleman, and the Queen's head had been omitted from his drawings. Marr takes up the tale: 'For forty minutes or so, Benn seems to have done all the talking, and left the Palace believing the Queen agreed with him, or at least would not confront him.' He was now 'convinced that if you went to the Queen to get her consent to abolish the honours list altogether she would nod and say she'd never been keen on it herself and felt sure the time had come to put an end to it'. Marr wrote, 'Many people have left the Queen's presence, before and since, having mistaken her cautious politeness for agreement.' He added that 'her private office went quietly to work on Harold Wilson and the civil service. Benn's own civil servants more or less ignored his plans. In July, the Queen's Private Secretary, Sir Michael Adeane, told Benn she was "not too happy" about a set of six Battle of Britain stamps with her head missing from five, and Benn made a small tactical retreat, "in view of the bad press I'm getting".'[103]

This is doubtless all accurate. A small addendum to the incident might, conceivably, be of interest to the philatelically minded. On one of her visits to Oxford, Princess Margaret told those with whom she was dining that the Queen did not trust her own judgement in aesthetic matters and always showed designs for new stamps and coins to her mother and sister. In 1965, when the Benn–Gentleman proposals for the Battle of Britain stamps were shown to the Queen Mother, she was adamant that they should be rejected, reminding the Queen, 'You are the Head of *State!*'[104]

The Queen Mother once went out to dinner in London during a week when there was an exhibition at the National Portrait Gallery of portraits of the Queen. Someone asked if she had seen them. 'I have not been to the exhibition, but I have seen most of the pictures, I expect,' replied Her Majesty. 'There have been no nice portraits since Annigoni, and that is for two reasons. One is that the Queen is devoid of egotism, so she does not care about how they depict her; the other is that she has no aesthetic sense – as she'd be the first to admit – and so she does not notice that they are all bad paintings.'[105]

Some years later when the tiny, splodgy portrait of the Queen by Lucian Freud went on display at the Queen's Gallery, one of her courtiers, an acquaintance of mine, found a friend staring at the picture quizzically. 'Even she noticed it was hideous,' said this loyal courtier. 'I ventured, however to say to her – Well, there is one thing, Ma'am, at least he hasn't—'

'I thought of that,' the Queen had quickly interrupted. 'He might have painted me in the nude.'[106]

9

'REMEMBER.'

CHARLES I'S LAST WORD

On the last day of her state visit to Germany, 26 June 2015, the Queen, with Prince Philip, visited the Second World War concentration camp Bergen-Belsen, where tens of thousands of prisoners had been killed – among them, the diarist Anne Frank. They passed the mounds which contained mass graves – over 20,000 bodies. The Queen was eighty-nine, her husband ninety-four. Both had been alive during the war, her husband, at its close, serving in the Royal Navy, she in the ATS. They walked vigorously up the long path to the camp, and they spent quite some time in silence. Afterwards, when various elderly people had been presented to the Queen, both camp survivors and former British servicemen who had helped to liberate the camp, her minders told her it was time to leave. She did not do so at once. Instead, she paused, and asked if she could spend a few more moments of reflection.

Such a place cannot fail to stir profound emotions. Naturally, it would have been moving, whichever world leader had visited the camp, and, especially, if it were one who lived through the horrific war which Hitler brought about. Nevertheless, there was a particular eloquence about this visit. The BBC commentator, when the report appeared on the television news, said, 'There was no pomp or ceremony; just a couple from the wartime generation taking their time to reflect and to pay their respects.'

It is clear what he meant, but this statement misses so much. They were not 'just a couple from the wartime generation'. As the British mockers never tire of pointing out, their Royal Family *is* German. Most of Prince Philip's extended family are German, he speaks German as fluently as he speaks English, and he descends directly from Queen Victoria's daughter, Princess Alice, the Grand Duchess of Hesse-Darmstadt.

Queen Elizabeth II became the Queen because, in the second decade of the nineteenth century, a German Prince named Leopold, from the Franconian Duchy of Coburg, had been married to Princess Charlotte, daughter of the Prince Regent of England. Although King George III had fifteen children, and innumerable illegitimate grandchildren, it had begun to look as if none of his descendants would produce a legitimate heir. Princess Charlotte, unlike her father, was extremely popular in Britain, and all hopes for the future of the monarchy hung upon her and her handsome young German husband. In 1817 Charlotte gave birth to a son who was dead, and she herself died a few hours later.

There followed the strange scramble during which Charlotte's uncles abandoned their mistresses and tried to produce a legitimate heir instead. The uncle who won the race was the Duke of Kent, who married Prince Leopold's sister, Princess Victoire, originally of Saxe-Coburg-Gotha. Her daughter, Alexandrina Victoria, became Queen Victoria, who did not merely rescue the British monarchy, but became the mother and grandmother of so many of the royal dynasties of Europe: the grandmother of both the Russian Empress, whose murder we remembered in the opening paragraphs of this book, and of the German Emperor, Wilhelm II, in whose arms she died on the Isle of Wight in 1901.

What we call the First World War could be seen, in its origins, as, among other things, an appalling family quarrel. The militaristic ambitions of Wilhelm II clashed with the Imperial power of Great Britain. (Look at a map of Africa in 1914 and then reconsider the sheer preposterousness of British fears about 'German imperialism': the land mass of the German colonies could fit into one tenth of the territory claimed by their supposedly decent, moderate British cousins.) Prussia had long regarded Russia as a rival in power, and resented its strength. So had Britain, but by the series of treaties and alliances into which sides had locked themselves, the European nations found themselves at war – on a superficial level, for the comparatively minor disturbances in the Balkans, and, a little later, because the Germans had invaded Uncle Leopold's kingdom, Belgium.

For, after Princess Charlotte died, Prince Leopold was made the first King of the new realm of Belgium. He had married a Princess of the Orleanist dynasty, and continued to exercise influence over the fledgling Victoria, and over his nephew, Victoria's future husband, Albert – also of Saxe-Coburg. (Albert was the son of Leopold and Victoire's brother, Duke Ernst I.)

Otto von Bismarck coarsely joked that Coburg was the 'stud farm of Europe', and he was right. Even before the 'stud farm' produced the future Queen Victoria, it had married into the Russian and Spanish royal houses. Almost more important, however, than the blood-line was the political idea which Coburg gave to Britain and to the rest of Europe. Prince Leopold's doctor and political adviser was the redoubtable Baron Stockmar. Between them, they looked at Europe post-1815. On the one hand, they saw the burgeoning Communist movement, which would very nearly bring successful revolutions to so many European capitals in 1848, which brought about the Paris Commune in 1870, and which would eventually topple the Imperial governments of Berlin and St Petersburg in 1917–18. On the other hand, they saw, after the fall of Napoleon, absolutist monarchism resurrected – in France, with the restoration of the Bourbons (this would last until 1830), and above all in Austria-Hungary.

Stockmar and Leopold felt that both forces – those of autocratic reaction, and those of Communistic revolution were potentially calamitous. They were liberals. They believed that it ought to be possible to develop a Parliamentary system of government modelled on the British one, only a Parliamentary system of government which would eventually evolve into the democracy which we enjoy today. It is surely no accident that the European countries where such systems have evolved most successfully, and without going through phases of fascist or Communist tyranny, have been the Protestant monarchies – Sweden, Norway, Denmark, the Netherlands and Britain. What was so distinctive and remarkable about Stockmar's vision was that he saw that it would be perfectly possible to retain a modified form of monarchy while Parliamentary democracy came into being. This was the vision of Britain, and of Europe, which Stockmar and Leopold gave to Prince

Albert. When Albert married Victoria, he taught the idea to her, and, when he died at the age of forty-two in 1861, she laboured to bring the idea to pass, not only in Britain but on the European continent. It was with this ambition in mind that she and Albert had begun to marry off their children to the daughter of the King of Denmark, to the son of the King of Prussia; eventually, other children would marry the heir of the Grand Duke of Hesse-Darmstadt in southern Germany, the daughter of a Tsar of Russia, and so on.

If Victoria and Albert's vision had been realized, there would have been no First World War. Their first-born daughter Vicky, who became the German Empress, was married to a man who entertained liberal views, and who would never have pursued the hawkish policies of his son, the aggressive Wilhelm II. Alas, Fritz – Wilhelm's father Friedrich Wilhelm, who ruled as Friedrich III from March to June 1888 – died of throat cancer aged just fifty-six. His father had lived to ninety. Had Fritz lived so long – until 1922 – Prussia might well have evolved into a more liberal place, in which Parliamentary government put a check on the militarists. Fritz would never have gone to war with his cousins Nicholas II of Russia and George V of Britain.

The dark, spectral wraith of all this history followed the old couple who walked up the path to Bergen-Belsen.

That was what made it so moving, and so unlike 'just a couple from the wartime generation'. They were incarnations of what Germany might have been... Had the Emperor Friedrich III not had throat cancer, had Nicholas II and Alicky (Prince Philip's great-great-aunt) not had a haemophiliac child, and not fallen prey to the pathetic delusion that he could be cured by Rasputin... It was the war provoked by Elizabeth and Philip's cousin Wilhelm II and the revolutions which followed that led directly to the rise of Hitler, to Belsen and to Auschwitz, to the tens of millions of deaths of the twentieth century. The alternative to despotisms or revolution, which was Baron Stockmar's benign vision, was there, incarnate, a sad old lady and her husband, walking up the narrow path towards the last resting place of Anne Frank.

Four years earlier, the Queen visited the Republic of Ireland. She was the first British monarch to do so – the last time a monarch had set foot on Irish soil had been a century before, when King George V went to what was then Kingstown and is now Dun Laoghaire. There were the inevitable protests by Sinn Fein and others, but the overwhelming majority of Irish people were moved by the royal visit. In a way which was comparable to her visit

to Bergen-Belsen, it meant so much, not because it was a
British Head of State visiting the Republic, but because
it was her. Her grandfather, 'Grandfather England', had
been King during the Troubles. The monstrous history
of the English in Ireland is carried by a monarch, for a
monarch carries with her many generations – whereas a
politician can only represent his or her own generation.
At the state banquet in Dublin, the Queen – it had been
her own idea to do this – began her speech, 'A Uachtarain
agus a chairdre' – 'President and Friends' in Erse.
President Mary McAleese exclaimed, 'Wow!' three times,
as the assembly burst into applause. Almost as eloquent
as this gesture was the Queen's silence, the humility of
the bowed head in the Garden of Remembrance.

After the Queen's state visit, everyone knew that the
Troubles were indeed over, and that whatever crimes
and horrors were committed from now on, there was no
going back to the state of near civil war which, for thirty
years of the Queen's reign, had raged in the island of
Ireland: in the North, of course, but also on occasion
in the Republic. The Queen was not able to forget the
murder of her husband's uncle Lord Mountbatten and
his family. It was all the more remarkable that, in the
June following her visit to Dublin, she met the Sinn
Fein Deputy First Minister of Northern Ireland, Martin
McGuinness, and shook his hand. Sinn Fein had refused

to have any part in her visit to Dublin, but McGuinness's handshake was an admission of how badly he and his colleagues had misread the situation.

In both these cases, gestures of great symbolic significance could have been enacted by elected politicians. Of course they could. One remembers Nixon in China. A monarch, however, is different. The thing which makes them so unacceptable as Heads of State to republicans is the very reason they are such eloquent figures in the life of a nation – eloquent not in what they say but in what they are. Why should X or Y be King or Queen 'just' because their father was King Somebody? That is the apparently reasonable republican question. The answer is that they are carriers of the past, often of the buried, unremembered or half-remembered past. They are bearers. The Queen was not simply the British Head of State. She was also the bearer of her father's national leadership in the war, of George V's salvation of the modern monarchy, of Edward VII's genial, if catastrophic, wish to extend *Entente* throughout Europe (placing alliance and treaties with France above his family ties in Germany). She was the bearer of the legacy of Queen Victoria, who, with Prince Albert, pioneered the modern idea of constitutional monarchy. She was the bearer of all the past history of the British Isles: of her ancestors the Hanoverian dynasty, and of the resistance to it by her other ancestors the Jacobite Pretenders. She was the bearer of the Scottish Unionists of Crown and Parliament, and of the Jacobites who rebelled against the English Protestant Germanic Whig hegemony. She was the bearer of all-but-forgotten memories of our Civil Wars. No other being, except the one who had inherited the throne, could possibly exercise this symbolic function.

This is at no time so poignantly clear as on Armistice Sunday, when, with representatives of all the armed forces, and of the political parties, and of those who are still involved in armed conflict in different parts of the world, the sovereign remembers the nation's dead. Every nation remembers its dead in ceremonial ways. As Prince Philip told Jeremy Paxman in an interview, 'Any bloody fool can lay a wreath at the thingummy.'[107] There is, however, surely something of extraordinary potency about the appearance of the British sovereign as she appears at the Cenotaph in Whitehall each year. She carries the past.

Year by year at Whitehall, she is the first to carry the wreath in remembrance of the war dead. All the dead seem to be there, including the dead of the Civil Wars, and of her own ancestor Charles I who was beheaded just yards away from the site of the Cenotaph.

By the nineteenth century, the British sovereign retained the right to advise and caution her ministers, but power had passed out of her hands. This was something which Queen Victoria on occasion behaved as if she had forgotten. The more tactless of her politicians, most notably Gladstone, rather enjoyed reminding her that she was no longer able to exercise power. The more beguiling of her ministers, such as Benjamin Disraeli, flattered and cajoled her, most notably when he encouraged her to style herself the Empress of India. But Queen Victoria was in essence politically astute, and she knew that the sovereign could not, and should not, exercise real power. The influence which Stockmar and Prince Albert had conceived as being a sovereign's proper role could not, indeed, be exercised if the sovereign had power in the overt sense of the word.

Victoria's highly amusing, and long-suffering, Private Secretary, General Sir Henry Ponsonby, was often the go-between who had to spell out the limitations of royal influence. A bone of contention was often the armed services. The Queen's cousin, the Duke of Cambridge, was for many years the Commander in Chief of the British Army, and he and Queen Victoria both deeply resented the military reforms of the Liberal politician Edward Cardwell. Ponsonby quite often found himself being asked by the Queen's sons, especially by Prince Alfred, Duke of Edinburgh, and Prince Leopold, whether it was the Minister for War or the Queen who controlled the Army, seemingly unaware that this matter – as Ponsonby put it – 'had been settled by the late Charles I'.[108]

Charles I, notoriously, raised an army against his own people, and it was upon this charge that he was tried and found guilty, paying with his head. It was mischievous of Ponsonby to mention that unfortunate monarch, however, since – as the Victorian Liberal Party knew very well, and resented – the Royal Family continued to exercise considerable influence in military matters well into Victoria's reign, even if, technically speaking, it was the War Office which held the purse strings and made the ultimate decisions.

Charles I, who stepped out on to the hastily constructed scaffold on that freezing 30 January 1649, died a martyr's death. His statue, at the south side of Trafalgar Square, looks down Whitehall – the scene of his death – towards the Victorian House of Commons.

At the beginning of her superb book, *The Trial of Charles I*, C.V. Wedgwood wrote, 'the conception of monarchy for which King Charles both lived and died has vanished from the earth. Where the institution survives today, it does so in a form that he would not recognize.'[109]

This is true. If it were wholly true, however, and if absolutely *nothing* survives of the concept of monarchy since the days of the Royal Martyr, then is it not the case that Britain does not really have a monarchy any more – rather, an hereditary presidency, or, even more derisory, a pretend monarchy? Modern monarchists often like to quote the Victorian constitutional wizard Walter Bagehot – 'We must not let in daylight upon magic' – to justify the keeping of the Royal Life a little bit secret. Nothing wrong with this, but the phrase can sometimes put one in mind of the scene in the film *The Wizard of Oz*, when the 'Great Oz' turns out to be simply an old man hiding behind a curtain and trying to project a magnified version of his voice and face upon a credulous world. Not a very bad man, as Dorothy Gale calls him, just a very bad wizard.

Bagehot's phrase about 'magic' suggests that if we saw too much of the Royal Family we should not be able to believe in monarchy. Many members of the public in 1969, who had sat through the film of *The Royal Family*, probably thought this. It must, however, be remembered that Bagehot, as well as being a constitutionalist, was also a journalist. And journalists always like gossip about royalty. It sells papers. They therefore have a tendency to concentrate on the gossip and 'miss the many-splendoured thing'. That 'thing', for a small minority of monarchists today, is a religious concept, a sense that the monarch is indeed 'the Lord's anointed'. For a much larger number of monarchists, however, it is also something much more obvious, and less contentious: a continuation of history, a link with the nation's past, both remembered and, almost more important, forgotten.

The Establishment dresses up the individual who has inherited the role in a crown and with ceremonial roles, but it is they, the people of influence, the elected dictatorship of the political classes, the civil servants, the politicians, the quangos, the journalists, the Vice-Chancellors and the Chattering Classes who exercise power and influence in the land; and it is the Prime Minister who exercises all the real power. That is the view of things which we considered in the last chapter, and which was championed by Tony Benn. It is the view which inspires idealistic republicans to wish to rid us of the undignified spectacle of someone who happens to be the heir to a long royal line from enacting a farce: reading a 'Queen's Speech' which has been written by the Government, appointing generals and judges and bishops who have been chosen by the Establishment, and for the rest of the time appearing, sometimes in ceremonial costumes to please the tourists, and sometimes merely going through the motions, supporting charities, visiting schools and hospitals, laying wreaths at the memorials for wars in which most of the people who died had not wanted to fight.

Of course, to keep the 'magic' element of monarchism, it is necessary to protect the person of the monarch, and not to expose them to constant press scrutiny. At the same time, there is truth in what Queen Elizabeth II is herself quoted as saying – 'I have to be seen to be believed.' If she had not been prepared to spend so many days of her life on parade, visiting every corner of the Commonwealth, as well as of the United Kingdom, tirelessly going through her ceremonial duties, laying foundation-stones, cutting ribbons, releasing bottles onto the prows of ships, there would have been irresistible calls to abolish the monarchy. (They were all but irresistible when Queen Victoria refused to go through these ceremonial and public duties.)

But when a monarch is 'seen to be believed', it is not the same as when a politician or a pop star is seen. When the Pope appears in public, he does so not as an individual, but as the inheritor of the Fisherman's Ring. The Popes go back in a (more or less) unbroken line to the Apostle who was told by Jesus Christ, 'Upon this Rock I will build my Church.' That is what the crowds go out to see.

In a comparable way, that is what the crowds go out to see when the British Queen is on parade. They are not going to see Elizabeth Windsor, a dutiful public servant with an interest in horses. They are going to see an embodiment, not of 'magic' or fantasy, but of an historical reality. The Pope, whether or not you believe in God (let alone Roman Catholicism), really is, historically, the successor of St Peter. The Queen, whether or not you approve of the fact, really is the descendant of William the Conqueror.

When she was crowned in Westminster Abbey, in a ceremony which still, when you watch it, has the power to electrify the viewer, she was taking upon herself the mantle of the past.

We began this short book recalling the murder of the Queen's cousin the Emperor of Russia, and the deposition of her cousin the Emperor of Germany; we recalled the extremes of political horror which were suffered by countries such as Russia and Germany, when they replaced Queen Elizabeth II's relations with governments which were headed, eventually, by Joseph Stalin and Adolf Hitler. It was suggested that those who found George V and his stately wife Queen Mary a little less than interesting would much prefer to be in a country of which they were the titular Heads of State than to live under the monster-dictatorships.

It may be a point too easy to make. Clearly, other factors – economic factors, primarily – can be adduced as reasons why Britain did not find itself, in the 1930s, dotted with a Gulag Archipelago, nor ruled by Nazis. Had Britain lost the First World War, had its economy suffered as Russia's and Germany's suffered, it would have taken more than Queen Mary, in her prettily veiled toque, delighting the crowds at the British Empire Exhibition at Wembley, or George V shooting industrial quantities of Norfolk pheasant, to prevent a brigand dictatorship occupying Whitehall.

Yet, I should like to end this book by suggesting that the monarchy is a little more than might appear to be the case by a glib rehearsal of arguments for a republic. Before we end, we should answer some rather simple questions. What does a monarchy supply which a republic does not? And, more specifically, what has the subject of this short book brought to British public life, which an elected President would not have been able to do?

For, the Queen, in her own person, is the best argument for monarchy. Her way of conducting the monarchy over the last sixty years is itself an argument which outshines the apparently reasonable demands of republicanism.

In his diaries, there is a touching moment – 31 May 2007 – in which Tony Benn noted, '*The Guardian* this morning published a poll of its readers, who had nominated the "greatest Britons" of the last fifty years. John Lennon came top, Barbara Castle came ninth and, believe it or not, I came equal twelfth ahead of Churchill and Ted Heath and the Queen herself, who were equal thirteenth. It is a quite extraordinary turn-up for the book.'[110]

The Guardian began its history as *The Manchester Guardian*, a Liberal newspaper so staunchly puritanical that it used to refuse to report the racing results. It was therefore unlikely ever to have been Elizabeth II's favourite reading. The paper now is what would be called Centre-Left in politics. It is possible that a similar poll, conducted among the readership of a Conservative newspaper, would place the Queen above John Lennon, as one of the 'greatest Britons'. In a sense, however, it would not affect an argument for monarchism if she was still level-pegging with Ted Heath at equal thirteenth, or even if she slipped down the scale with lesser mortals. Fervent monarchists sometimes spoil their case by hero-worshipping the occupant of the throne, or claiming what can only be true of infallible beings or fantasy figures, that she has 'never put a foot wrong'. What could that mean, and how, if it meant anything, could it be true of *anyone*? If the system is worth defending, it would not matter precisely who was the constitutional monarch, so long as they performed the functions with a modicum of dignity, did not involve themselves in party politics, or scandalize public opinion by gross behaviour. In this sense, George V's example, of being as dull as possible, was a good one to follow. The monarch should not be 'popular' in the sense that a crooner or an actor is 'popular'. Confusion arose during the lifetime of Diana, Princess of Wales because she was a superstar, who was enormously venerated and loved in her own person. In this, she was enjoying the sort of public esteem offered to heroines – Marilyn Monroe, or Mother Teresa. Public feelings about her were worlds away from what most people felt about Queen Mary or Elizabeth the Queen Mother. When she died, therefore, in horrific circumstances – but also, tragically and confusingly, the sort of death which one expects not of royal personages but of superstars – the reaction was similar to the public feeling when Elvis Presley or John Lennon died.

The Royal Family, during the last few decades, were given painful lessons, by the press and the public, about what happened when they antagonized public opinion. The scenes in the Mall during the week following the death of Princess Diana took the Queen's closest advisers by surprise. They were ringing up newspaper editors in despair, saying, 'Tell us what to do!'

'WHERE IS THE QUEEN WHEN THE COUNTRY NEEDS HER?' was the banner headline of the Rupert Murdoch-owned *Sun* on 4 September 1997. The next day, the Queen flew south to London from Balmoral, and broadcast to the world, from Buckingham Palace. You could see, through the window behind her, the long street lined with an extraordinary display of makeshift shrines to her daughter-in-law's memory. Outside Kensington Palace, where Diana had lived, mountains of flowers piled up. One of Diana's friends said to me during that week, 'The Queen is respected, but not loved. Diana was loved.'

During the interview given to announce their engagement, Prince Charles had stood beside a winsome, shy young Diana and been asked whether he was in love with his fiancée. He replied, 'Whatever love means.'

Ever since Diana's friend told me the Queen was respected but not loved, I have thought about those words, and felt there is something wrong with them, even though I knew what he meant. 'Respect' is too cold a word to describe what the Queen, through a very long period of time, and over a vast global spectrum, has inspired.

Thomas Carlyle, the Victorian sage, gave a series of lectures entitled 'On Heroes and Hero Worship', the last of which was on 'The Hero as King'. The 'Kings' whom he most admired were Oliver Cromwell and Napoleon – 'our last great Man'.

Tony Benn, scanning *The Guardian* and being proud that he was a 'greater Briton' than the Queen, might well have thought that this was what being a monarch meant – being a 'great man' or a 'great woman'. Since monarchs are not given power any more, and since the power of the Crown in fact resides with the Establishment, there would surely be a case for discarding the monarchy altogether.

That would definitely be true, were it an accurate picture of what constitutional monarchs, as pioneered and developed by King Leopold and Queen Victoria, and Prince Albert, actually were. They are more than simply figureheads, more than simply pieces of artificially constructed 'magic', to render elected governments more poetic. They are symbols, it is true, and the symbolism is deep. They are symbols of an unchanging presence in a changing world; symbols of the continuing past;

symbols of a power which is not entirely invested in the politicians who so ardently desire it; symbols, indeed, of a power which no human being is entitled to exercise, and which will always elude them in the end.

The ceremonies which surround the State Opening of Parliament make this abundantly clear. At first, the doors of the Commons are shut against the intrusion of their sovereign, as they were shut against Charles I at the beginnings of the Civil War. Then, the members of the Commons troop through to the Second Chamber to hear the 'Queen's Speech'. Yes, everyone knows that the words of this document have been penned by the elected Government of the day. But the ritual of the Crown coming to the Lords reminds everyone present that Power itself, that nebulous but recognizable thing, is not the possession of political parties or of individuals. If the Queen for some reason is unable or (as was so often the case with Queen Victoria) unwilling to attend the State Opening, the Crown is still carried in procession to the Lords. Power is Elsewhere. Power is not the Possession of one person or one party. That is surely a magnificent thing to enshrine into a constitutional ritual, and it is not possible to envisage how that would be enshrined in a republic.

Britain has changed more in the last seven decades than at any previous period in its history. Technology, and the arrival of the Internet; immigration, and the transformation of all large British cities, but most especially the Capital; the decline and change of British industry; the decline and change of British influence in the world; the increase of secularization; the change in the class system; the alteration in sexual *mores*; all these things make the Britain of 2016 a place which the British of 1952 would find scarcely recognizable. Since that time, one thing, and one thing only, has remained constant, and that is the monarchy.

Great movements, like the Labour Party or the Trade Union movement, no longer attract the huge following they used to; membership of organized religions is in steep decline; there are fewer and fewer things in British life which bind people together.

'WHERE IS THE QUEEN WHEN THE COUNTRY NEEDS HER?' asked *The Sun* on one very sad day in the autumn of 1997. The answer could be – at the State Opening of Parliament, every time it happens; at the Cenotaph every year remembering the nation's dead; at the Trooping of the Colour every summer; at garden parties in Buckingham Palace and at Holyrood meeting a wider range of the public than any politician ever does. Over the last sixty years the Queen, when she was 'needed', has been to every corner of the globe, sometimes, as at Commonwealth Government

Leaders' Conferences at moments of crisis, assuring the governments of Africa and Asia that a benign interest is taken in their affairs, regardless of what the politicians may say; and in many non-Commonwealth countries, the Queen's visits have supported British interests, commercial and political, while signalling that Britain and the British are more than the political parties they happen to vote into office. Where was the Queen when her country needed her? She was actually there – on the streets of London, staring with grief and wonder at the mounds of flowers for Diana, following the state funeral for the much-adored Queen Mother, receiving foreign Heads of State as various as American and European Presidents, African democrats and demagogues, Arab Kings and Communist Chinese dictators. When Bobby Moore, the England captain, collected the Football World Cup in 1966, he did so from the hands of the Queen; when the people of Aberfan wept for their dead children in 1968, they did so in the presence of the Queen, just as when the schoolchildren of Dunblane were massacred in 1996, the Queen wept with their parents. At dozens of excruciating Royal Variety Show Command performances at the London Palladium theatre, the Queen and her husband have sat patiently while comedians made supposedly cheeky jokes about them, and as crooners stretched the meaning of the phrase 'easy listening'; when James Bond visited the London Olympic Games in 2012, he did so with a guest appearance by the Queen. Church Synods have been inaugurated, many a ship has been launched, foundation-stones have been laid for libraries, universities, schools, all by the Queen, just as she has visited factories, hospitals and broadcasting stations. As far as light can be shed on the matter, the only place she has refused to visit is Battersea Dogs' Home – the pathos.

Had hers been an impossible act to follow, then all her tireless self-application, all her dutifulness, would have been double-edged. It is not impossible, though. She has been humble enough, for the most part, simply to go through the motions. Her absence of scintillating small talk has become a national joke – 'Have you come far?' 'What is it you do?' No one minds. No one wants her, or has ever wanted her, to be a comic turn, or an orator who kept dinner tables in fits of laughter. Not that she is humourless. As the years have passed, people have become more and more aware that the cold-seeming eye which she casts on events is often amused. An Edinburgh resident said to her that she must be relieved that they had demolished the brewery next to Holyrood Palace, so that when she stayed in the city she would no longer have to breathe in the smell. 'Yes,' she agreed, 'but you realize that is where they have built the new Scottish Parliament, on the site of the brewery? We don't get the smell, but we get a lot of hot air.' In her Jubilee year, all those who had served as her page gave her luncheon at a gentlemen's club. One of them had the daunting task of escorting her into the billiard room, playing the piano and singing what were supposed to be her favourite numbers from *South Pacific*. Some days later, she ran into Lord Airlie, her former Lord Chamberlain. 'I gather my son was entertaining you the other day, ma'am.' 'Trying to,' was the clipped reply.[111]

Si monumentum requires, circumspice. Sir Christopher Wren's monument in St Paul's suggests that those who would seek his monument should simply look about them. By a similar token, ask what a constitutional monarch should be like – and look at Elizabeth II. She is, and has been, the embodiment of what the position requires. Of course, not every constitutional monarch could have had her good fortune of being blessed with a sturdy temperament, good physical health and a long life. The longevity has undoubtedly made her even more successful at her task. So has the frequent stiffness of her manner, and the continued mysteriousness of what is going on behind her face.

She has demonstrated time and again, and in so many different areas, what a monarch can do. The 'magic' of which Bagehot spoke is not something tinselly and sentimental, nor is it simply a fake dressing-up of an Establishment puppet. It is palpable. The crowds who have appeared at her Jubilees have been bigger and more enthusiastic than anything seen in modern British history. Whatever love means, this woman is loved.

NOTES

CHAPTER I

1   Humphrey Carpenter, *Robert Runcie: The Reluctant Archbishop* (Hodder & Stoughton, 1996), p224.

2   Rodney Brazier, 'The Monarchy' in *The British Constitution in the Twentieth Century*, edited by Vernon Bogdanor (published for the British Academy by Oxford University Press, 2003), p72.

3   Harold Nicolson, diary entry 17 August 1949, *Diaries and Letters, 1907–1964*, edited by Nigel Nicolson (Weidenfeld & Nicolson, 2004), p367.

4   Kenneth Rose, *George V* (Weidenfeld & Nicolson, 1983), p317.

5   Rose, p395.

6   British Pathé, http://www.britishpathe.com/video/king-george-v-jubilee-speech-aka-george-5th/query/george+v+silver+jubilee (accessed 11 March 2016).

7   G.R. Searle, *A New England? Peace and war, 1886–1918* (Clarendon Press, 2004), p422.

8   Brazier in Bogdanor, p72.

9   Marion Crawford, *The Little Princesses* (Cassell, 1950; Duckworth, new edition 1993), p31.

10   Ibid.

11 *The Oxford Book of Satirical Verse*, edited by Geoffrey Grigson (Oxford University Press, 1980), pp371–2.

12 Brazier in Bogdanor, p78.

13 Ibid.

14 Ibid.

15 'Death of King George V', *Continual Dew* (London, 1937).

CHAPTER 2

16 Sarah Bradford, *Elizabeth: A Biography of Her Majesty the Queen* (Heinemann, 1996; Penguin, revised edition 2002), p345.

17 Ben Pimlott, *The Queen: Elizabeth II and the Monarchy* (HarperCollins, Jubilee edition 2012), p407.

18 Interview with Kenneth Rose, quoted Pimlott, p407.

19 Nicolson, diary entry 21 March 1949, p366.

20 Pimlott, p238.

21 The royal spelling of 'Mummie', which most English-speakers spell 'Mummy', seems to be of a piece with the pre-1914 diction of the old Queen Elizabeth, which both her daughters inherited.

22 Hugo Vickers, *Alice: Princess Andrew of Greece* (Hamish Hamilton, 2000), pp124–5.

23 Nicolson, diary entry 21 March 1949, p365.

24 Vickers, p225.

25 *Guardian*, 22 December 2007.

26 Ibid.

27 *National and English Review*, August 1956.

28 Private information.

29 Crawford, p78.

30 'Crawfie' spells her nickname 'Alah' and the Royal Website spells it – rather boldly these days – 'Allah'.

31 Crawford, p71.

32 Hensley Henson, *Retrospect of an Unimportant Life*, vol. III (Oxford University Press, 1950), p281.

33 Bradford, p106.

34 Bradford, p71.

CHAPTER 3

35 Phil Dampier and Ashley Walton, *Prince Philip: Wise Words and Golden Gaffes* (Barzipan Publishing, 2012), p103.

36 *Radio Times*, 6 February 2012.

37 Bradford, p114.

38 Bradford, p248.

39 Kitty Kelley, *The Royals*, p134.

40 Dampier and Walton, p37.

41 Dampier and Walton, p73 and passim.

42 Pimlott, p269.

43 Gyles Brandreth, *Philip and Elizabeth: Portrait of a Marriage* (Century, 2004), p377.

44 *Telegraph*, 23 October 2006.

45 Brandreth, p349.

46 Vickers, p273.

47 Vickers, p397.

48 Vickers, p259.

49 Philip Eade, *Young Prince Philip: His Turbulent Early Life* (HarperPress, 2011), p21.

50 Bradford, p178.

51 Bradford quoting from Alistair Horne, *Harold Macmillan, Volume II: 1957–1986* (Macmillan, 1989), p170.

CHAPTER 4

52 Carpenter, p71.

53 Vickers, p419.

54 Carpenter, pp221 ff.

55 Carpenter, p224.

56 Roy Strong, *Coronation: A History of Kingship and the British Monarchy* (HarperCollins, 2005), p435.

57 *Daily Telegraph*, 18 November 2013.

58 National Secular Society website, 9 February 2105.

59 Strong, p486.

60 The Queen's Christmas message, 2011.

CHAPTER 5

61 Brandreth, p205.

62 Bradford , p167.

63 BBC News Website, 22 February 2006.

64 Bradford, p444.

65 *The Times*, 12 February 2016.

66 Private information.

67 Pimlott, p381.

68 Bradford, p479.

69 Quoted in Bradford, p166.

70 *Guardian*, 12 July 1997.

71 Sue Townsend to author.

72 Andrew Marr, *The Diamond Queen* (Macmillan, 2011), p297.

73 Elizabeth Longford, *Royal Throne: The Future of the Monarchy* (Hodder & Stoughton, 1993), p167.

CHAPTER 6

74 T.S. Eliot, *For Lancelot Andrewes* (Faber & Gwyer, 1928).

75 Philip Larkin, *The Complete Poems* (Faber & Faber, 2012), p116.

76 Pimlott, p446.

77 Pimlott, p445.

78 Tony Benn, diary entry 4 May 1977, *Conflicts of Interest: 1977-80* (Arrow, 1991), p127.

79 Pimlott, p343.

80 'I Shall Vote Labour', published in the *New Statesman*, 1966.

81 Elizabeth Longford, *Elizabeth R: A Biography* (Weidenfeld & Nicolson, 1983), p278.

82 Bradford, p413.

83 Pimlott, p416.

84 Pimlott, p399.

85 Bradford, p381.

86 Private information.

87 Pimlott, p465.

88 Pimlott, p117.

89 Harold Macmillan, *Pointing the Way: 1959–1961*
    (Macmillan, 1972), pp471–2.

90 Bradford, p123.

91 Peter Oborne, *The Triumph of the Political Class*
    (Simon & Schuster, 2007), pp192–3.

92 Bradford, p250.

CHAPTER 7

93 Dampier and Walton, p46.

94 Bradford, p175.

95 Bradford, p132.

CHAPTER 8

96 C.V. Wedgwood, *The Trial of Charles I* (Collins, 1964),
    p223.

97 Acceptance speech, Australian of the Year, 25 January
    2016.

98 Ibid.

99 Quoted in Pimlott, p670.

100 Caroline Ellis and Minna Thornton, *Women and Fashion:
    A New Look* (Quartet, 1989), p152, quoted in Pimlott,
    p659.

101 Pimlott, p658.

102 Marr, p208.

103 Marr, p210.

104 Private information.

105 Private information.

106 Private information.

CHAPTER 9

107 Dampier and Walton, p67.

108 William M. Kuhn, *Henry and Mary Ponsonby: Life at the Court of Queen Victoria* (Duckworth, 2002), p205.

109 Wedgwood, p9.

110 Tony Benn, *More Time for Politics: Diaries 2001–2007* (Hutchinson, 2007), p45.

111 Private information.